Quick-to-Listen
LEADERS

where life-changing ministry begins

D1042660

Group

Loveland, Colorado
www.group.com

Quick-to-Listen Leaders
Where Life-Changing Ministry Begins

Visit our Web site: **www.group.com**

Credits
Senior Acquisitions Editor: Brian Proffit
Chief Creative Officer: Joani Schultz
Editor: Jennifer Root Wilger
Copy Editor: Lyndsay E. Gerwing
Art Director: Granite Design
Print Production Artist: Granite Design and John Mestas
Cover Art Director: Jeff A. Storm
Cover Designer: Alan Furst Inc.
Production Manager: Peggy Naylor

Unless otherwise noted, Scripture taken from the HOLY BIBLE, NEW INTERNATIONAL VERSION®. Copyright © 1973, 1978, 1984 by International Bible Society. Used by permission of Zondervan Publishing House. All rights reserved.

Scripture taken from *THE MESSAGE*. Copyright © Eugene H. Peterson, 1993, 1994, 1995. Used by permission of NavPress Publishing Group.

Library of Congress Cataloging-in-Publication Data
Ping, Dave.
  Quick-to-listen leaders : where life-changing ministry begins / by Dave
Ping and Anne Clippard.-- 1st American pbk. ed.
    p. cm.
  Includes bibliographical references.
  ISBN 0-7644-2661-3 (pbk. : alk. paper)
  1. Pastoral theology. 2. Listening--Religious aspects--Christianity. I.
Clippard, Anne. II. Title.
  BV4011.3.P56 2004
  253'.7--dc22
                                        2004018862

10 9 8 7 6 5 4 3 2 1   14 13 12 11 10 09 08 07 06 05

Printed in the United States of America.

DediCATION

To the glory of God, with grateful recognition of Rich Walters, Gary Sweeten, Larry Chrouch, Hal Schell, Edith Barr, and all the quick-to-listen leaders who paved the way for us. And in memory of Anna Louise Telfair, whose will to grow for ninety-three years continues to bear fruit for God's kingdom.

AcknowLEDGMENTS

We want to acknowledge the many wonderful people who've inspired and challenged us. First and foremost, we want to thank God for our spouses, Pam and Bill, for decades of patient attentiveness, persistent thoughtfulness, and tenacious encouragement. The richness of their love saturates each day of our lives, and we hope some of it has spilled over onto the pages of this book.

We thank God for both our natural and church families and for their unwavering support. Friends from College Hill Presbyterian Church, the Vineyard Community Church, and Winton Community Free Methodist Church have fed and clothed our spirits for many years. Very special thanks go to Anne's "Heart Sisters" Bible study group for more than twenty-five years of prayers, accountability, and faithful friendship. Thanks to Sue Baker, Rita Hauck, Janet Johnson, Lynne Ruhl, Sue Wade, and Lynn Wheeler for steadfast care and honesty through countless trials and joys.

Thanks also to our editors, Jennifer Root Wilger, Candace McMahan, Brian Proffit, and all the wonderful people at Group Publishing for believing in this book and for all their work in helping it become a reality. Special thanks to Jean Coakley for her invaluable help in tracking down several difficult sources (and, more important, for being Dave's mom).

Finally we wish to give special thanks to the board of trustees, staff, and volunteers of Equipping Ministries International for supporting us and encouraging us in this project, for being living examples of all we teach and write, and for laboring to bring the ministry of Christ-centered listening and relationships to the church around the world.

Table of **CONTENTS**

"The man who plants and the man who waters have one purpose, and each will be rewarded according to his own labor. For we are God's fellow workers; you are God's field, God's building" (1 Corinthians 3:8-9).

Listening
WORKS!

H ere's a message for all leaders who want to expand God's influence in their cities, neighborhoods, or churches: Listening works!

For nearly twenty years, we have traveled the world as spiritual planters, helping leaders sow millions of tiny seeds of God's kindness in their own communities. Wherever we go, we encourage leaders to use simple acts of service to show God's love and draw people to Jesus. We also tell the folks we train that they have to learn the practical art of being "quick to listen and slow to speak." Why? We've found that *seeds of kindness don't grow well without the water of listening.*

Our friends Dave Ping and Anne Clippard have given us powerful relational tools that help stir the seeds of kindness into vibrant life. Their simple, doable, and humorous approach to listening has not only touched the two of us in our family and personal relationships but also helped thousands of other pastors, missionaries, and group leaders in more than fifty countries! Years ago we began integrating the teaching you'll find in *Quick-to-Listen Leaders* into the heart of Vineyard Community Church, the fledgling congregation we were planting in Cincinnati, Ohio. Over time these listening and relational skills have shaped our identity as a church body and greatly multiplied our effectiveness in the community.

At our church we have a saying: "When you invite the city to church, *the city comes to church.*" Since our early days, we've invited an incredibly diverse crowd of people to come and discover a new kind of church experience in which whoever you are and whatever you've done, you can come "just as you are and be loved." At the Vineyard, it's not unusual to see a corporate CEO in an expensive suit sitting next to a biker covered in tattoos. Such diversity sounds exciting, and it is, but it can also be very messy if you don't know how to handle it. And, to be honest, we really didn't.

As we sought to meet the conflicting needs created by these vastly different backgrounds, we experienced constant misunderstanding. In addition, false assumptions about others' motivations created all sorts of conflicts. Leaders were burning out quickly. One of Vineyard's greatest "God breakthroughs" came when we connected with Dave and Anne. We explained our situation, and they agreed to come in and teach *all* our leaders—from church secretaries to recovery group leaders to pastoral staff—how to be quick to listen and slow to speak.

We wanted everyone at Vineyard to show love and acceptance to each broken, hurting person who came in our door. As a church, we wanted to meet drug abusers, unemployed people, doctors, lawyers, or schoolteachers in the midst of their struggles and show them the way out. We thought we could do it all, but we were wrong. Learning to be quick to listen and slow to speak healed us of the mistaken notion that it was our job to be people's saviors and to provide them with all the smart spiritual answers they needed for personal healing. Instead, we learned to come alongside folks on a more equal footing, to befriend them, and to help them find real answers from the only true Savior.

Learning to listen sounds like a simple, obvious thing, but it was a huge leap forward for us. The listening skills we learned from Dave and Anne came to us at a very strategic point in the life of our church. These skills arrived just in time to save us from many bad habits that, left unchecked, could have destroyed both our fellowship and our outreach. Implementing the skills described in *Quick-to-Listen Leaders* enabled us to develop into a community of grace and acceptance and laid the foundation for our expanded outreach to the city of Cincinnati.

We are excited that Dave and Anne are bringing the life-changing message of *Quick-to-Listen Leaders* to a broader church audience. For us, for countless Vineyard staff and volunteers, and for thousands of other Christians around the globe, the practical ideas contained in this book have been a powerful antidote to the disease of poor listening that keeps church leaders ineffective and drives hungry people away from God.

May this book help us all learn to use our ears more than our mouths and to show God's kindness by truly listening to those around us. We want to thank Dave and Anne for taking the time to listen and invest in us over the last fifteen years. We hope and pray that God will use *Quick-to-Listen Leaders* to bless countless others in the same way.

Steve and Janie Sjogren
Founders, Vineyard Community Church
Cincinnati, Ohio

"My dear brothers, take note of this: Everyone should be quick to listen, slow to speak and slow to become angry, for man's anger does not bring about the righteous life that God desires" (James 1:19-20).

1

You Have to BE QUICK

That's right; you have to be quick! In the animal kingdom and in God's kingdom, you're always pursuing something or being pursued. Your enemy is constantly close on your heels "like a roaring lion looking for someone to devour" (1 Peter 5:8). Your good works and the abundant fruit of God's work through you are continually at risk to a thieving predator waiting for any opportunity to "steal and kill and destroy" (John 10:10). We're not saying this to scare you. As a Christian leader, you already know it's important to be on your toes against the wiles of Satan and to be swift to pounce on the spiritual opportunities the Holy Spirit sends your way. You know that, spiritually speaking, slowpokes don't usually prosper. So why this book?

There are lots of books on the market today about being quick to adjust to the rapidly changing cultural landscape in which we find ourselves. The brilliant scholars and innovative leaders who write these books advocate becoming proactive trend-watchers and courageously reshaping our churches and ministries to meet tomorrow's challenges. They promote bold, new organizational models and up-to-the-minute mission strategies. They propose radical ideas for changing the way the church does business. Do we really need another one of these books?

In some ways *Quick-to-Listen Leaders* is one of those books, and in some ways it's not. The radical leadership ideas we will promote are not new; they come from leaders who died more than 1,900 years ago. Nevertheless, even in the midst of the sweeping cultural and religious changes we face today, they are genuinely powerful and literally life-changing.

We will present not a new congregational or organizational model but something more personal and, in our experience, much more potent in empowering growth and bringing healthy change to your church. We're not going to talk about being quick to reorganize or quick to adopt some groundbreaking new program. No, our message is much more basic than that. Our goal in *Quick-to-Listen Leaders* is to help you and your followers learn to live out twelve simple words of advice from one of the New Testament's most forthright and forceful leaders:

"Be quick to listen, slow to speak and slow to become angry."

Our friend Bill Lowrey currently serves as the Director of Peacemaking and Reconciliation for World Vision International. Before joining World Vision, Bill witnessed the power of these twelve words when, as a missionary, he was given his first assignment in peacemaking: to travel to the African nation of Sudan and try to help two tribes, the Dinka and the Nuer, make peace after more than eight ruinous years of war. Several teams of international mediators had already tried and failed, so as he entered this volatile situation, Bill realized that to bring peace, he'd have to do something out of the ordinary. He decided that his first job was to be quick to listen and slow to speak.

As Bill sat down with tribal leaders and members from both sides, he realized that the American and European habit of doing things by the clock was counterproductive. The constantly changing pressures of day-to-day tribal life just weren't compatible with Western-style negotiation approaches in which meetings started at 9 a.m., broke for lunch at noon, and ended at 5 p.m. This just wasn't how these folks operated. For them, no communication of great consequence could take place at the kinds of meetings the previous negotiators had tried.

Big decisions customarily required big events, and the primary means of transmission for important ideas was elaborate storytelling.

After much listening and consulting with tribal leaders on both sides, Bill helped them set up a suitable event that culminated with the chiefs of the Dinka and the Nuer tribes sitting and hearing each other's stories. Seated across from each other, they began to tell their tales, one at a time. The one speaking could talk for as long as he wished without being interrupted. The other chief agreed to listen, without interrupting or arguing, knowing he was going to get the same opportunity.

The chiefs spent three whole days telling story after story of their pain, their suffering, and the sacrifices they'd made because of the war. Although there were many tense and painful moments, by the end of the three days, both were able to acknowledge the suffering each tribe had experienced from the atrocities committed by the other. Finally, after each had listened and spoken, and listened and spoken again, they were willing to talk about forgiveness and to work together for peace.

After the peace pact was signed, one smiling chief approached Bill and thanked him, saying he'd attended numerous fruitless peace talks arranged by the United Nations but this was the first time he had been allowed to tell his story and really felt heard. Many might seek peace and even pursue it, but Bill agrees with the book of James that being quick to listen is the best foundation.

The radically humble and stunningly simple words of James 1:19 have changed our lives and the lives of the tens of thousands of leaders and ordinary Christians our ministry has equipped around the world.[1] These words are an essential part of a larger collection of practical leadership advice that James delivered to the rapidly expanding network of churches that were spreading the brand-new message of Jesus "among the nations." Like every fledgling movement, the early church was struggling to figure out the norms of behavior that would allow its members to thrive and overcome external and internal threats to its survival. Sound familiar? Read on.

There were plenty of high-powered personalities among the early church leaders—people who thought it was their job to talk and their followers' job to listen and obey. Perhaps that's why James started the passage by saying, "My dear brothers, take note of this: Everyone should be quick to listen." If James were speaking to us today, he'd probably say something like, "OK, ladies and gentlemen, pay close attention. Everybody, and I mean everybody, leaders and followers alike, *absolutely must* learn to shut up and *really* listen before you start shooting off your mouths (or 'be quiet and really listen before you speak,' in Anne's more genteel version). For us, listening is job number one!"

> *Then a great and powerful wind tore the mountains apart and shattered the rocks before the Lord, but the Lord was not in the wind. After the wind there was an earthquake, but the Lord was not in the earthquake. After the earthquake came a fire, but the Lord was not in the fire. And after the fire came a gentle whisper. When Elijah heard it, he pulled his cloak over his face and went out and stood at the mouth of the cave. Then a voice said to him, "What are you doing here, Elijah?" (1 Kings 19:11b-13).*

Listening for a Still, Small Voice

What's full of more raw energy than a tornado, more powerful than an earthquake, and more formidable than a forest fire? Anyone who has read the story of Elijah knows the answer is "a gentle whisper from the mouth of God."

For those of us who are pursing God's call on our lives and who—like poor, old Elijah—are being pursued by an army of worries and demands that threaten to do us in, listening seems like the least of our concerns. Like Elijah, we've experienced those days when everything just clicked—times God showed up and it all flowed miraculously into place. We've also seen times nothing seemed to work at all, and we've gone from ecstasy to despondency overnight.

We've also probably all had our moments of crying out, "I have had enough, Lord!" While others simply relax and go about their business, we've felt weighed down with heavy burdens of responsibility. We've been constantly conscious of how what we do or don't do will impact many lives besides our own. And in these challenging moments, of course, there have been plenty of well-meaning advisers ready to tell us to have faith or "don't worry, be happy!" or that we should delegate more of our responsibility to others. Unfortunately, these are often the very same people who've demanded *our* heads when things went wrong or when someone to whom we've delegated responsibility dropped the ball.

Even if we've never cried out like Elijah and begged God to take our lives, there have probably been many days and nights when we've desperately needed a gentle whisper from on high. But the whispered word from God cannot help us unless we hear it—unless we are *quick to listen.* It's our first job as Christian leaders. Like it or not, we don't know where we are going unless God tells us, and we can't truly know how to encourage, inspire, or guide others unless we really learn to use our ears. Perhaps instead of *looking* for demographic portents and signs of the times in the whirlwinds, earthquakes, and fires of our culture, it's time to quiet our own inner voices and listen for a change.

You'd think we'd get this obvious message. God created each of us with two ears, two eyes, two nostrils, and thousands of sensitive nerve cells covering every centimeter of our skin. Then he cunningly formed our brains so we could interpret the incoming data from all of these sources. God gave us the gift of language and the ability to decipher what others are saying to us. He painstakingly designed us so we can focus outwardly, to pay attention to him and to the world and the people around us. Considering the amount of trouble to which God went to give us these capacities, they must be really important. So why do human beings seem to be so much better at *not* listening and *not* paying attention than anything else?

As we teach leaders about the power of listening, we use a simple, four-minute exercise to demonstrate this fact. We call it "Listen, Don't Listen." We ask participants to pair up with one other person and take turns telling each other something exciting or frustrating that's happening in their lives. For the first minute, we ask the people who are listening to do everything they can think of to *show* the ones who are speaking that they genuinely care and are interested in what the speakers are saying. After a minute, we have them trade roles and repeat the process.

Even after twenty years of teaching, we're still surprised by how well most of our students are able to listen when they put their minds to it. They consciously adjust their seating, posture, and body language. They try to use good eye contact, lean forward to show interest, and nonverbally encourage their partners to relax and tell their stories. Soft tones of considerate conversation fill the room. Afterward, the speakers almost universally respond by saying they enjoy the feeling that comes with being so conscientiously understood and cared for by their listeners.

In the second part of the exercise, we ask our students to repeat the process—only this time while the speakers tells their stories, we ask the listeners to do everything they can think of to show they *aren't* really interested. The tone of the conversation starts out the same but quickly escalates into nervous humor, restless frustration, and often real anger. It's not unusual to see some of the speakers actually walk away from their non-listening partners in disgust. After less than a minute of having everything they say discounted, even though they know it's just an exercise, the speakers begin tapping into personal reservoirs of unpleasant memories they've cataloged under the word *disrespect*. When we ask the speakers how they feel, it's very common for them to say it feels "normal" to not be listened to. (This response is especially common from the married couples we ask.)

When we invite the people who were not listening to tell us how doing this felt, some say they feel *mean* intentionally ignoring people. Others say it feels more natural and far easier to blow people off than to listen to them. Many even admit to relishing the experience of expressing what our friend Dr. Paul Meier calls "the hidden jerk within." [2]

The entire exercise would be pretty funny if it weren't so tragic. But the fact is that even when we do understand right and healthy and loving ways to act toward others, we routinely *choose* to do just the opposite. This is especially true when it comes to listening. It's very hard to find a leader who will come out against compassionate listening. We all know it's a good thing—like prayer or motherhood or tithing—but in our daily lives, many of us approach it with all the enthusiasm a hyperactive two-year-old has for bedtime. We know listening to our followers and our families is good for us and good for them. It's even good for our health, but so are liver and lima beans or broccoli and brussels sprouts. The truth is that listening is a very good thing that many of us *would much rather avoid*.

> The truth is that listening is a very good thing that many of us *would much rather avoid*.

Reasons We Don't Listen

Why don't we listen? Our ministry teams have traveled around the world and taught listening to leaders from more than fifty countries. From Nepal to Nigeria, Cuba to Canada, Australia to Austria, we've found the same things. When leaders are being completely honest without being diplomatic, they will usually admit to having some of the following beliefs about listening.

> **1.** Listening takes far too long.
>
> **2.** Listening makes us look weak, indecisive, or wishy-washy.
>
> **3.** Listening muddies the water with too many emotions and opinions.
>
> **4.** Listening slows down the implementation of our plans.
>
> **5.** If we listen to suggestions and don't use them, people get mad at us.
>
> **6.** If we listen to people, they will assume we agree with them.
>
> **7.** We're not really interested in hearing opinions that disagree with our plans.

If any of your objections are on this list, or if you have your own unique list, don't worry. We know that listening is difficult, and we'll take a more detailed look at the reasons in later chapters. For now, suffice it to say that listening doesn't come naturally and isn't easy. There are a hundred reasons we avoid it. Listening may be one of those things Jesus was referring to when he said, "With man this is impossible, but with God all things are possible" (Matthew 19:26).

Why might listening seem impossible? Because whoever and wherever we are, good listening highlights this very unpleasant fact: Though we leaders like to think of ourselves as competent, intelligent, and in control, our human limitations smack us right in the face when we honestly listen to the hearts of others.

Most people don't like the feeling this gives them.

> Though we leaders like to think of ourselves as competent, intelligent, and in control, our human limitations smack us right in the face when we honestly listen to the hearts of others.

Real listening requires a level of sacrifice. It means dying to ourselves and our agendas. Listening also teaches us humility by confronting us with the embarrassing reality of how little we actually know and how little power we truly have to change other people's lives.

To truly listen is to open the door to a very frightening place. Listening can propel us through the curtain that leads to a kind of relational holy of holies. It's a place we fear to tread, knowing that we are men and women of "unclean lips." It exposes pain, shame, vulnerability, and humanity. In our hearts, we're deeply afraid of the power of the uncomfortable things God might reveal through what is whispered here.

It's not easy to listen to others. But, on the other hand, wherever we've gone in the world, we've found an insatiable hunger among leaders and followers alike. They want to be heard! They're desperately looking for people who not only *know how* but *choose* to overcome the inner obstacles that keep them from listening. They want to find listeners who will take off their shoes as they tread on the "holy ground" of others' inner lives. We're not just talking about the *active listening* skills you've been exposed to in college or seminary counseling courses. We're talking about a kind of listening that is the very life of leadership. It isn't merely active; it's *proactive*.

To be quick to listen, we have to override natural tendencies and bad habits we've developed over the course of our lifetimes. We have to take the initiative to listen *before* the need is obvious and pressing. We have to exercise our listening muscles and reinforce healthy, new habits to the point where our *first* impulse becomes seeking to understand before being understood. Quick-to-listen leaders are people who are working to get ahead of the curve. Quick-to-listen leaders seek out those who need to be heard instead of waiting for them to request an audience in their offices. Quick-to-listen leaders wait to speak the truth at the right time and in the most loving way possible.

▌▌▌ Had Enough?

Like you, our friend Steve is a leader who has faced lots of trials and seen "heaps of miracles" since he answered the call to become a pastor. After coming to Cincinnati, Steve spent nearly a year meeting face-to-face with over 2,000 people and inviting them to the first service of the new church he and his wife were planting. On the first Sunday, only twenty-seven people showed up.

Imagine how dispiriting it was to see less than 1.5 percent of the thousands he'd invited respond. But after a few years, things had changed dramatically. Over 4,000 more worshippers now joined the twenty-seven souls who'd attended that first service—and more than 50 percent of these folks were new Christians! By the early 1990s people were traveling from around the world to come see how Steve and Janie had done it.

Once a part-time school bus driver and unpaid pastor, Steve was now leading one of the fastest growing churches in America. He had gone from preaching in one sparsely attended service, where you could almost hear crickets chirping in the background, to directing seven packed and rocking worship celebrations each weekend. The number of ushers showing people to their seats far surpassed what would have been the total attendance just a few years ago. You'd think Steve would be pretty content with all of this, but, in fact, on the Monday morning this story begins, he was ready to quit.

A gentle voice in the back of his head seemed to be whispering, "What are you doing here, Steve?" Steve wondered what this was about. His ministry seemed to be going extremely well. More people were coming to Christ and being baptized every week. His writing was receiving international recognition. He was getting speaking invitations from churches all over the world. Lately, however, he found himself dreaming of quitting the ministry and doing almost anything else—even selling used cars was starting to look good.

As he often does when he needs to think, Steve got in his old truck and went for a long drive. Spilling out the troubled contents of his heart to God, Steve expressed how inadequate he felt with the overwhelming needs people were bringing to him as a leader. It wasn't just the couples struggling with their marriages, the ministry team leaders who couldn't seem to get along, or the angry folks blaming him personally for policy decisions that impacted their lives. It was the combined pressure of all the needs of all the broken people who seemed to think he should have all the answers.

"God," Steve prayed, "I don't know what to say to all of them! I've tried to cast the vision you've given me, but let's be honest, Lord—the people you're sending me are annoying! They just don't listen! And I'm sick of trying to get through to them!"

As Steve calmed down a little from what was for him a fairly typical rant, he felt a painful and sobering thought percolating up from somewhere deep in his spirit. With a sigh of self-accusation, he uttered the words that were brewing inside: "Maybe I just don't have a pastor's heart."

All this soul-searching was making Steve a little hungry, so he pulled into a Taco Bell drive-through to get something to eat. In the silence between shouting his order into the microphone and picking up his food, God spoke to Steve. It wasn't an audible voice; it was a nearly imperceptible mental whisper.

"Steve," it said. "Open your door. I have a present for you."

Feeling a little silly, Steve stopped the car and opened his door. Ground into the pavement below was a scarred and tarnished penny. "Gee...thanks..." was the sarcastic thought that went through his head as he dug the practically worthless coin from the soft asphalt. But then God's quiet voice spoke again.

"In the world's eyes, the people I'm sending you are like this penny. They're flawed, imperfect, and forgotten. Even churches don't see much value in wasting time on them. In some eyes, they may look shabby and worthless, but to me, they are just like you, Steve. They're precious beyond measure!"

Tears streaming down his face, Steve drove home with a penny, a bag of burritos, and a whole new understanding of the incredible value God places on the broken, bothersome, infuriating people we all are.

"It's a funny thing," Steve remarked several weeks after this happened. "Since that Monday morning, as I've been tempted to get angry or blow people off with a few brief words, I'll look down on the ground and find another penny. I now keep a whole stack of them on my desk to remind me of God's generous heart and of the special calling he's placed on my life. I still don't have many answers, but I'm trying hard to pay attention to people and show them God's love by giving them plenty of time to talk. I'm not that good at it yet, but I'm working on becoming a pastor who listens."

Quite a few Monday mornings have come and gone since Steve first told Dave this story. On many of them, though weekend church attendance now approaches 7,000, Steve still loses patience with people and feels like quitting the ministry. But now whenever Steve says, "This is it. I'm really quitting this time!" his wife, Janie, smiles, gives him a hug, and says, "Bring me a bag of burritos on your way home."

The Call of the Quick-to-Listen Leader

Now let's talk about you. For some reason you've picked up this particular book at this moment in time. We don't know why. Perhaps it had something to do with the phrasing of the title. Maybe a friend, a teacher, or a member of your congregation has recommended it to you. And maybe, in addition to any or all of these reasons, you are responding to the quiet inner prompting of the Holy Spirit similar to what Steve experienced on his expedition to Taco Bell.

You've been tapped to be a leader. You've been called out and chosen. It may not have been as dramatic as what happened to Moses at the burning bush or Paul on the road to Damascus, but in its own way, it is no less miraculous or intimidating. If you are reading this now, it's likely that God has called (or is at this very moment calling) you to step forward into a more fruitful kind of leadership than you've known or experienced before—the kind of leadership that recognizes the value of flawed, imperfect, forgotten people and, with God's help, transforms them and raises them up to serve.

> If you're starting to feel even a little bit hypocritical preaching about balanced priorities and making time for family, you're reading this book just in time.

You may be leading in a congregation, in a parachurch ministry, on a board of elders, in a women's or men's small group, in a Christian business, or in the secular arena. Wherever you are called to serve, we believe that the time you invest in reading the pages ahead holds the promise of many fresh insights and more than a few divine appointments in the days to come.

You may already be a successful leader. Our guess is that you didn't pick up this book because you're failing. On the contrary, your successes may have produced a ravenous organizational monster that requires constant attention and feeding. If you are like most successful leaders we've met, this "achievement monster" is probably well on its way to devouring all the time and energy that you need to stay healthy and sustain your relationships with God, family, and friends. If you're starting to feel even a little bit hypocritical preaching about balanced priorities and making time for family, you're reading this book just in time. The handwriting is already on the wall, and it says, "It's time to be quick to listen and quick to equip fresh teams of listening leaders to help you carry the load."

You may be at a crucial stage in your personal or organizational growth at which you just can't afford to waste any time on fruitless misunderstandings and unnecessary conflicts. You want to maximize the time you have for building your team and accomplishing the vital tasks God has set before you. The stakes are high. Gone is the time you could afford to be sloppy in your relationships with those you lead. Now you are sensing a need to become more focused, more intentional, and more present to the people you serve.

You may have realized a need to reach out and encourage others to become more authentic. If you want to *be real* with people and help them *get real* with God, themselves, and each other, the pages ahead will provide a valuable road map and some road-tested vehicles that can help take you there. You'll learn to travel farther down the road to Christ-centered community and genuine teamwork than ever before and, in the process, to raise up generations of healthy new leaders who can do the same for others.

If God has been convicting you of a need to go deeper with him, to experience richer connections with those you love, and to pursue more fruitful relationships with those you lead, you're reading the right book.

> There are thousands if not millions of problems that leaders face every day of the week, but in our experience there are only a few real solutions.

We're especially excited to be writing to leaders who are courageous and humble enough to face their own weaknesses and shortcomings so that the people in their care might experience an environment in which they can truly receive the dreams and desires of their hearts. God has used servant leaders like you to bring wholeness and healing to our lives. So we'd like to return the favor by sharing the principles, processes, tools, and habits that God has used in our lives so you can experience more of what the Lord has in mind for you and your followers.

We think the message of this book will resonate with the part of your heart that drew you into ministry in the first place. Though as a leader you're called to help others shoulder their burdens, we believe the pages ahead will show you how to lay down huge loads of unnecessary anxiety and heavy responsibility that don't belong to you. To every pastor who has accepted God's commission to present the Word of God in its fullness, to every missionary who longs to reveal the glorious riches of Christ to a waiting world, to every leader who has stepped forward to proclaim him, admonish, teach, or administrate in his name, this book is for you.

Instead of adding more demands to the already insurmountable expectations your followers so readily place on you, we hope to give you easy-to-follow directions to a place where you'll receive more compassion, more understanding, and more respect than ever before. We want this book to become a pathway to a more fulfilling and effective ministry that is wholly biblical, nuts-and-bolts practical, and led by the Holy Spirit.

There are thousands if not millions of problems that leaders face every day of the week, but in our experience there are only a few real solutions. The good news of this book is that with God's help, those few solutions can help you immensely in working through most if not all of the problems with which you deal.

This is a book about learning to listen to God, your own heart, and the hearts of the people you've been called to lead. It's about connecting with everyone in your life in fresh ways that not only bring hope, encouragement, and insight but also point the way to a deeper relationship with Jesus. Practicing the spiritual disciplines found in James 1:19 is much more powerful, more genuine, and more in-tune with the Spirit of Christ than any mere *technique* you've learned or any *academic model* you've been taught. It's not really a technique at all; it's the power of a new kind of relationship that brings the compassionate heart and listening ear of Jesus into the difficult, day-to-day work of encouraging and equipping others in the work of ministry. You will learn how to

▌ overcome natural confusion, misunderstanding, and conflicts;

▌ get rid of the dangers inherent in reactive and passive listening;

▌ become a more Christlike active and proactive listener;

▌ ask great questions that help people go deeper in their discipleship;

▌ confront and work through relational problems before and after they erupt into catastrophic conflict;

▌ overcome five listening barriers that prevent you from dealing with the real issues;

■ evaluate how your leadership temperament affects the way you listen; and

■ improve your ability to listen to God, your culture, and your church.

All this starts right where you are now and leads to a place of greater teamwork, deeper community, and more fun than you've ever associated with the "L word" (listening) before. So let's "put our ears on" and get started listening for that still, small voice that makes all the annoyances and challenges of leading so incredibly worthwhile.

ENDNOTES

1. Our ministry is Equipping Ministries International, Inc. (EMI), a Christ-centered, nonprofit, interdenominational ministry dedicated to "equipping ordinary people for life-changing ministry." EMI has focused on a few biblically sound solutions that address a wide variety of potential problems in every aspect of life and ministry. In addition to the listening and speaking-the-truth-in-love skills discussed in this book, we've developed training solutions that equip leaders and lay people to replace distorted thinking with biblically sound beliefs; use focused prayer to overcome spiritual bondage, past traumas, and unhealthy relational patterns; and reach out evangelistically in attractive and nearly irresistible ways. You can contact EMI at our Web site, www.equippingministries.org, or by calling (513) 742-1100 or 1-800-EMI-GROW toll-free in the U.S.A.

2. Paul Meier, *Don't Let Jerks Get the Best of You* (Nashville, TN: Thomas Nelson, Inc., 1993).

▌▌▌ Are You Quick-to-Listen? ▌▌▌

If you're not sure what kind of listener you are, we've included a simple listening inventory. The following twenty statements pertain to how others might experience you as a listener. Use the scale provided to rate your listening habits as you think your spouse, family members, or the friends and colleagues who know you best would most likely describe them. If you're really brave, photocopy this page, pass it out to three or four people you trust, and let them fill it out for you.

_____ **is a person who**
(Write your name here.)

1. gets impatient and annoyed when others express opinions that don't agree with his or hers.

   (1) practically never (2) very rarely (3) sometimes (4) frequently (5) almost always

2. genuinely welcomes the opportunity to hear ideas, suggestions, and constructive feedback that could help his or her personal effectiveness.

   (1) almost always (2) frequently (3) sometimes (4) very rarely (5) practically never

3. fidgets with objects, taps his or her hands or feet, or looks at the clock while others are speaking.

   (1) practically never (2) very rarely (3) sometimes (4) frequently (5) almost always

4. takes plenty of time to consider what others are thinking and feeling before responding to what they say.

   (1) almost always (2) frequently (3) sometimes (4) very rarely (5) practically never

5. mentally checks out and stops listening when people don't get to the point as quickly as he or she would like them to.

   (1) practically never (2) very rarely (3) sometimes (4) frequently (5) almost always

6. communicates that he or she is interested by maintaining good eye contact and exercising open, friendly body language as others are talking.

   (1) almost always (2) frequently (3) sometimes (4) very rarely (5) practically never

7. spends more time formulating his or her responses than actually listening.

   (1) practically never (2) very rarely (3) sometimes (4) frequently (5) almost always

8. prepares to listen by removing anything that might distract him or her or create a barrier for those with whom he or she will be talking.

   (1) almost always (2) frequently (3) sometimes (4) very rarely (5) practically never

9. changes the subject when a conversation begins to touch on emotional issues or when he or she doesn't like the direction it is going.

   (1) practically never (2) very rarely (3) sometimes (4) frequently (5) almost always

10. accepts people first and then gets to know them rather than prejudging them based on how they look, talk, or what others have said about them.

(1) almost always (2) frequently (3) sometimes (4) very rarely (5) practically never

11. minimizes or discounts the opinions, experiences, and feelings of those with whom he or she disagrees.

(1) practically never (2) very rarely (3) sometimes (4) frequently (5) almost always

12. stays engaged in conversations and relationships even when they become difficult or uncomfortable.

(1) almost always (2) frequently (3) sometimes (4) very rarely (5) practically never

13. pontificates, lectures, or engages in long-winded monologues when it would be wiser to listen.

(1) practically never (2) very rarely (3) sometimes (4) frequently (5) almost always

14. acts proactively in seeking honest input from those on whom his or her decisions or actions will have substantial impact.

(1) almost always (2) frequently (3) sometimes (4) very rarely (5) practically never

15. uses the silent treatment and/or other forms of emotional blackmail to get his or her way or to get even with people who have displeased him or her.

(1) practically never (2) very rarely (3) sometimes (4) frequently (5) almost always

16. tests his or her understanding of what others say by paraphrasing what they've said and repeating it back to them.

(1) almost always (2) frequently (3) sometimes (4) very rarely (5) practically never

17. postpones necessary but unpleasant conversations or avoids them altogether.

(1) practically never (2) very rarely (3) sometimes (4) frequently (5) almost always

18. initiates conversations with people who he or she believes might be upset with him or her to hear what is on their minds.

(1) almost always (2) frequently (3) sometimes (4) very rarely (5) practically never

19. acts in ways that discourage people to approach him or her and say what's on their minds.

(1) practically never (2) very rarely (3) sometimes (4) frequently (5) almost always

20. demonstrates a healthy sense of humor about his or her mistakes, foibles, and shortcomings.

(1) almost always (2) frequently (3) sometimes (4) very rarely (5) practically never

▪▪▪ Overall Rating ▪▪▪

Now, on a scale of one to ten with ten being "practically perfect" and one representing "very poor," rate this person's day-to-day performance in carrying out the biblical command to be "quick to listen, slow to speak and slow to anger."

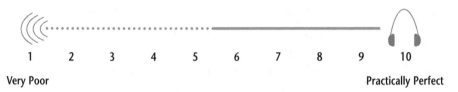

| 1 | 2 | 3 | 4 | 5 | 6 | 7 | 8 | 9 | 10 |

Very Poor   **Practically Perfect**

▪▪▪ Scoring ▪▪▪

As you took the inventory, you probably noticed that the odd-numbered questions focus on actions that get in the way of good listening and the even-numbered responses focus on helpful listening behaviors. To find your quick-to-listen score, total the numerical values for all of your odd-numbered responses and subtract them from the total of your even-numbered responses.

For example, if your even-numbered responses add up to 42 and your odd-numbered responses add up to 35, your total score will be 7.

```
Even    42
Odd    -35
        7
```

Slow—A score of zero or below indicates that, like many leaders, you are much quicker to speak than to listen. Read and practice what you learn in the upcoming chapters to get into a serious listening training regimen.

Steady—A score of between 1 and 10 indicates that you are beginning to pull ahead of many leaders in your listening skills. With a little more work, you could be a quick-to-listen contender.

Skilled—A score of 11 to 20 indicates that you have the skills to be a quick-to-listen leader. Be practicing them consistently, you will be a life-changer.

Quick—A score of 21 to 40 indicates that you are a terrific listening leader (if you are not being overly optimistic in your self-assessment).

No matter how you scored on this inventory, reading *Quick-to-Listen Leaders* will help you improve your ability to lead with greater compassion and power. It will also give you many practical insights and tools that will help you equip others to become more effective in life and ministry.

"Jesus took Peter, James and John with him and led them up a high mountain, where they were all alone. There he was transfigured before them. His clothes became dazzling white, whiter than anyone in the world could bleach them. And there appeared before them Elijah and Moses, who were talking with Jesus.

"Peter said to Jesus, 'Rabbi, it is good for us to be here. Let us put up three shelters—one for you, one for Moses and one for Elijah.' (He did not know what to say, they were so frightened.)

"Then a cloud appeared and enveloped them, and a voice came from the cloud: 'This is my Son, whom I love. Listen to him!' " (Mark 9:2-7).

2

The Church You've
ALWAYS WANTED

When God talks, people listen. After hearing God's voice from a cloud, Peter, James, and John would probably be listening to Jesus a little more carefully. What about us? We may not have God's audible voice coming at us from the sky, but are we listening to Jesus? Carefully? If every follower of Jesus in your church read and obeyed every one of Jesus' teachings as they are recorded in the New Testament Gospels, Acts, and Epistles, what would that kind of church look like?

In *The Purpose-Driven Church*, Rick Warren tells us what he thinks we should see in a truly healthy church. He believes that when the leaders are leading and the followers are following Christ in the healthy, obedient ways that God intends, our congregations will grow like the church in Acts 2:42-47.[1] It's great to imagine!

If our congregations were growing like the early church, we'd be devoting ourselves to good teaching, to fellowship, and to prayer. We'd be constantly filled with awe at the many wonders and miraculous signs happening around us. We'd be sharing all we have with others and giving sacrificially to any who needed our help. We'd be so excited that we'd hardly be able to wait to get together and rejoice at the life-changing work the Lord was doing in our midst. It makes you want to say, "Amen!" and "Preach it, Brother Rick!" doesn't it?

> Our churches seem to be filled with incredibly self-centered and disobedient people, many of whom care more about the condition of the houses they own and the cars they drive than in the dilapidated state of their souls.

We've probably all dreamed of this ideal church. We want our churches to be vibrant and growing. But when we wake up, the reality is very different. Instead of a group of like-minded, Christ-following people learning and growing and sharing together, our churches seem to be filled with incredibly self-centered and disobedient people, many of whom care more about the condition of the houses they own and the cars they drive than in the dilapidated state of their souls. Over and over, our churches and Christian organizations run up against lethargy, conflict, and a "What's in it for me?" attitude.

Consider the experience of our friend Richard. Richard had been serving as senior pastor of the congregation described below for only a year when he realized that he was in the wrong place. He told us:

> *I knew that this church was what my seminary professors used to call a "do-over." They'd started out well, but in the last several years, they'd repeatedly blown it. When I arrived, there was still an atmosphere of smoldering resentment from past misunderstandings. But I believed that I'd handled tougher situations before and had the skills to bring about healing and renewed growth. By the end of the first year, I knew I was wrong, but my wife and I stayed on for another*

*four years. During that time I just accepted that my life was
going to be filled with constant tension and lots of ugly little
conflicts over apparently unimportant issues.*

*I tried to survive by lowering my expectations and working
hard not to let it get to me. I was going through the motions:
showing up for work on time, calling on people, cranking out
sermons, and delivering them on Sunday mornings. Outwardly I was passive, but inside I was dying. My prayer life
and my passion for ministry were practically extinct. By the
time the final conflict came, I was too bone weary to put up
much of a fight.*

How many of us can identify with Richard's experience? Does
our collective negative experience mean that the ideal of the New
Testament church has become truly unattainable in our day and age?
No! In fact, for anyone who hasn't given up and given in to the heartbreaking state of business as usual that's going on in so many of our
churches, it's a clarion call to find and fix the problems that are caus-
ing the disparity. Real listening can work miracles in strife-filled
churches. And it can start with you.

The Miracle Question

Back in the early 1990s, we attended a secular seminar by the
founder of a movement that was sweeping the counseling world.
Several studies had recently been published showing the ineffective-
ness of traditional, long-term, "problem-focused" counseling method-
ologies. In response to these studies, a family therapist named Steve
de Shazer[2] was promoting something he called "solution focused" or
"brief" therapies. One of the big ideas that came from this school of
counseling was a simple (and we think biblically compatible) technique called the "miracle question."

The concept is simple. When people focus on problems, all they
tend to see are the problems. The more they focus and dwell on the
problems, the more insurmountable the problems become. However,
when the same people begin to focus on solutions, even blatantly
miraculous ones, *they begin to see solutions.*

It's a bit like what Jesus said in Luke 11:34 about the eye being
the lamp of our body. When our eyes are *bad*, our bodies are full of

darkness. Interestingly enough, the New Testament word for *bad* in Luke 11:34 doesn't usually refer to a medical malfunction as we might think today. In biblical writings it is used almost exclusively to express the idea of *moral wickedness* or *evil*. When all we see is the evil of our problems, hope and light are eclipsed. But if we set our eyes on possibilities that are good and healthy, if we focus on "whatever is true, whatever is noble, whatever is right, whatever is pure, whatever is lovely, whatever is admirable" (Philippians 4:8), our whole body will be full of light.

> When people focus on problems, all they tend to see are the problems.

I don't know whether the family therapists at the conference we attended believed in literal miracles, but we certainly do. We've seen them over and over as we've taught in churches and mission groups around the world. We like to start one of our popular workshops for church leaders by posing our own version of the miracle question. Our miracle question goes a step further by encouraging people to envision how they might act, feel, and think differently if God showed up and miraculously solved their biggest problem. It goes something like this:

If Jesus miraculously got his way with you and the people you lead, what kinds of things might you see happening around you in the weeks, months, and years ahead? What would you be doing, and how would you be thinking and feeling differently?

Why don't you try it? Let your imagination run wild. Think about at least five positive things you would see happening if the Holy Spirit got loose in your neighborhood and you fully followed his lead. What successes or transformations can you imagine? What attitude adjustments or breakthroughs might you see? Use the work sheet on page 39 to record these thoughts.

When we ask church leaders to reflect on the miracle question, here are the things they envision:

We see our congregation praying, worshipping, and celebrating together like never before!

We see our auditorium full and spilling over with people who'd never darkened the door of a church before!

We hear the Word of God proclaimed so simply and powerfully that everyone wants to obey!

We hear people saying, "Look how those people love one another!"

We feel excited about reaching out and loving the people in our neighborhoods into relationship with Christ!

We're in awe as we constantly watch God healing and performing miracles among us!

We're thinking about more ways we can serve and accommodate all the people God wants us to reach!

We're thinking about how wonderful it is to follow Jesus and to dwell together in unity!

It's hard to read this kind of list without getting excited. *Wow* isn't a big enough word for responding to images and visions like these. These are visions deserving of serious exclamations such as "Hallelujah!" or even "Maranatha!"

Who would have thought such things were possible? It's exciting to imagine that miraculous changes like these can actually happen with God's help. If your list reflects even a little bit of God's love and truth, we believe he wants you to see the things you've written (and much more) come to pass in your situation. You've just started the process of developing a vision that is *so big* that it demands a miracle! Excited? You haven't even heard the best part. According to Ephesians 3:20, God is able to do "immeasurably more than all we ask or imagine, according to his power that is at work within us." So the outcomes God has in mind for you and those you lead are *even better* than anything you could write in answer to the miracle question.

A Dream of Quick-to-Listen Leadership

James 1:5 says, "If any of you lacks wisdom, he should ask God, who gives generously to all without finding fault, and it will be given to him." That's exactly what I (Dave) had been doing when I began to visualize my personal answer to the miracle question. (We say "visualize" because Dave is definitely a visual thinker. In fact, he can't hold a marker in his hand without producing some sort of chart or diagram.) As I listened to Dr. Larry Crabb speak about "Connecting in Christian Community," I was inspired by stories of Christian leaders and lay people experiencing deeper community. All through the seminar, I doodled away on his note packet. But I still didn't have a picture of what God wanted from leaders in the church.

The next morning I woke up with the words *seven circles of community* going through my head. I was intrigued by this enigmatic phrase and wondered what images might go with it. I drew seven big circles on a large newsprint pad. Ideas about what each circle represented just flowed. In a matter of minutes, I had completed the chart you see on this page. It brought together key concepts we'd been working on for several years and helped to describe some important answers to my own miracle question.

As you might expect, the key to the whole picture comes from James 1:19. These seven circles of community are only achievable when leaders become "quick to listen, slow to speak and slow to become angry." Each circle represents an essential piece that goes into making a truly healthy church, staff, or ministry team. None of these can happen without leaders who understand and practice proactive listening.

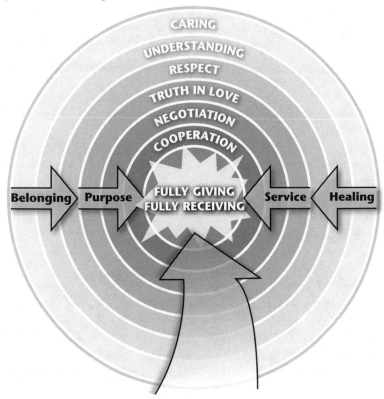

Quick-to-Listen Leadership

Think of each circle as a progressively higher and deeper level of leadership outcome. We'll briefly describe these seven outcomes here and then flesh out each one in greater detail in later chapters.

As the first circle shows, when leaders are quick to listen, they focus on creating an environment that clearly *communicates caring.* The oft-repeated cliché that "People won't care how much you know until they know how much you care" is far more than a clever saying. It is a stinging indictment of the cold, impersonal, know-it-all reputation that many churches and Christian organizations have earned in our society. We recently asked more than fifty ordinary people on the street what they thought of Christians. Most people responded with colorful adjectives such as *pushy, disrespectful,* and *judgmental.* Not a single one used the word *caring.*

We've made some real strides in the last decade or so, and things are beginning to change. But being seeker sensitive isn't the same as communicating genuine caring. A very intelligent young friend of Dave's summed it up well as he described why he was leaving a popular megachurch. This young man told Dave, "It wasn't that it *wasn't* caring, but it wasn't *really* caring either." Most people in today's churches demand leaders who genuinely care. They want to feel personally accepted and *really* cared for by their leaders. Genuine caring is not something that can be taught. You either care or you don't care. If you're in ministry, we hope you care, and we assume you do—but are you communicating that caring to your people? *Communicating the caring you do feel* is something every leader who wants followers needs to understand.

The second circle represents a place where *people feel truly understood.* As leaders we sometimes think *we* have a better grasp of the needs of our followers than they do themselves. However, unless we've taken the time to check in with each churchgoer personally, we're probably deluding ourselves on this point.

Consider Ingrid's story. Ingrid was head of the communications department in a medium-size Midwestern church. Bob, her senior pastor and direct supervisor, knew she was overworked and wanted to help her. He'd sensed their relationship was becoming increasingly strained due to busyness. (We're sure you can't relate to that.) So in order to "help" Ingrid, he started outsourcing some of her work. Unfortunately, the work he chose to outsource was the time-consuming but creative work that Ingrid loved most. So instead of helping matters, this action caused so much tension in their relationship that Ingrid finally asked an outside mediator to help them work things out.

To Bob's great surprise, Ingrid was irritated that he'd taken away the work that energized her most and given it to others. He was trying to be helpful, but by not communicating directly with Ingrid, he had nearly destroyed their working relationship. Toward the end of their mediation session, Bob asked, "How can I be more of an encouragement to you, Ingrid?" Ingrid answered that she missed the times they used to take a few minutes every week to have a cup of coffee and catch up. That's when Bob realized that a few minutes a week invested in listening could have saved him and his staff months of unpleasantness and fruitless misunderstanding.

It's tempting for us as leaders to assume that we know what is best for others. We may even make great sacrifices to try to help them. But here is the terrible truth: You can never understand what is going on in another person's heart without taking the time to listen. Listening is the closest you will probably ever get to walking a mile in another person's shoes. Without it, it's nearly impossible to build a bridge of understanding and cross over it into the real world of someone else's perceptions. For Ingrid and Bob, a little listening did much more than turn one staff relationship around; it made the church office a healthier place for everyone who worked there or passed through.

The third circle represents a place where *people feel deeply valued and respected.* Respect is probably the primary quality that makes would-be leaders into real leaders. People follow us when they sense that we value what they value or, at a deeper level, that *we value them.*

One associate pastor told us about a time his church was going through a staff change. Some of the things he heard from the personnel committee led him to believe that his days on staff were numbered. On the other hand, these same people were telling him how extremely important it was for him to be totally committed to the changes they were instituting. As you might imagine, these mixed messages led to feelings of confusion. It was hard for him to get motivated to invest time and energy into a ministry where his contribution didn't seem to be valued.

Eventually, the personnel committee called this pastor to express its faith in him. After this call, he was totally re-energized and was able to step out and truly lead as God had called him to do. He was no longer confused; now he felt valued. As a result, he was willing to commit his full efforts to his job.

When the people we lead experience the caring, understanding, and respect depicted in circles one through three, *outsiders* cease to be strangers and become more connected to our vision and the church's purpose. People who came in the door feeling vulnerable or wounded begin to feel safe and welcomed. Even if they've been burned other places, they can sense that this is a place where they can be themselves. They become *insiders* as they begin to experience more caring, more understanding, and more kindness and as they are folded into the life of the group.

The book of James underlines what is happening in these first three circles and sets up what will be happening in the next three: "You can develop a healthy, robust community that lives right with God and enjoy its results *only* if you do the hard work of getting along with each other, [and by] treating each other with dignity and honor" (James 3:18, *The Message*).

Feeling accepted, understood, and valued is so great in itself that we might be tempted to stop here, but even the most energetic Christian communities quickly deteriorate into feeble social clubs if they have no purpose beyond belonging. As the chart below

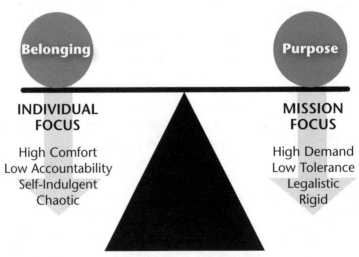

Balancing the Great Commission With the Great Commandment

demonstrates, too much focus on individual belonging leads to a culture that worships ease and comfort over hard work and productivity. Organizations that go too far the other way, toward purpose, usually become demanding, intolerant, and legalistic. We need to strike a balance between the sense of belonging we have inspired in the first three circles and the sense of purpose we want to create in the next three. We may start with meeting individual needs, but we must also move toward addressing a larger vision that will mobilize the entire community to obey the Lord's leading.

In 1981 our friend Ken was called to be chairman of the building committee at his church. He told us:

> As our committee began to work, we agreed that we would not proceed unless we sensed a true spirit of unity in the body. We started out very enthusiastically by obtaining a set of plans, presenting them to the congregation, and having the plans approved by a reasonable margin. The only thing that was missing was a sense of peace and unity in the body at large. There were some questions about where the money for missions or other projects would come from.
>
> Even though the vote had been favorable, the committee discerned that we did not have the unity we wanted. So we decided to respect the congregation by slowing down the process and taking two more weeks to listen to God and the people. After the two weeks, we decided to revise the budget to include both the building and extra money for missions. When the proposal was presented a second time, it was accepted with enthusiasm and with all the excitement and energy needed to make the project a success. This made me a believer in the importance of the listening process.

The fourth circle of listening leads us from belonging into purpose. In Ken's situation, Christlike listening enabled the church to move forward and further the Lord's purposes by constructing a new building. As Ken experienced, the way leading to purpose isn't always direct or obvious. It often requires stops and starts as leaders listen for

Too much focus on individual belonging leads to a culture that worships ease and comfort over hard work and productivity. Organizations that go too far the other way, toward purpose, usually become demanding, intolerant, and legalistic.

God's direction. As pastor Erwin McManus eloquently points out in his book *An Unstoppable Force,* "Before you can begin to call God's people to a new way of living and action, you must clearly establish for them the purpose for so painful a process." McManus goes on to say, "After you expound the purpose, you then expose the problems. There is no true leadership without facing problems." [3]

Exposing problems sounds like fun, huh? Not! Given the choice, most people would rather avoid dealing with even the most blatantly obvious problems. They don't appreciate people who point out the proverbial "elephant in the room." They'd rather blunder along, turning a blind eye to the people they hurt in the process. As leaders intent on following Christ, we can't afford this kind of selective blindness. If we see problems coming, we need to name them and face them head-on.

Ron, a volunteer church administrator, had been given the go-ahead to install a new computer system. Everything had been approved, but the delivery and installation timetable had not yet been set. Ron wanted to have a plan in place to inform the staff about the upcoming installation. He became concerned when he stopped by the church on a Saturday and saw the computer techs installing the new system. He was glad to have the new system installed but worried about the responses he would hear on Monday morning when the staff members turned on their computers to find a completely new and unfamiliar system.

Ron knew he was facing a potentially significant problem. He could have used the Saturday installation as an excuse for the apparent lack of communication. But instead he faced the problem and looked for a creative way to get everyone on board with a minimum of grumbling and irritation. Here's what Ron did.

Ron went home and found a bag of bows in his wife's Christmas decorations. He put a big bow on each computer. Along with the bow, he placed a letter explaining that the user was receiving a gift that would make his or her job easier and more efficient. The letter also explained that there might be problems or frustrations in learning the new system and included the name of a person who would be available to address these concerns.

It took a considerable amount of time for Ron to do all this. But it was time well spent. Because of Ron's consideration, the staff felt his respect and expressed real excitement and very little frustration about the new system.

Like Ron, leaders bring problems into the light, not with condemning announcements or dramatic trumpet flourishes but with "gentleness and respect." We are not the source of the truth we quietly make known, but we must be its champions. It is not enough just to listen; we must also learn to practice the skill Ephesians 4:15 calls "speaking the truth in love."

Unfortunately, "speaking the truth in love" is where many Christian leaders fall flat on their faces. We either don't do it or botch the delicate balance between honesty and tenderness. We fail to blend grace with truth, or we give in and start excusing sin. We have seen hundreds of examples of churches and Christian organizations that could not or would not or simply waited far too long to speak the truth in love. We have fallen into this trap ourselves over and over again. As McManus says, "Sometimes speaking the truth in love is so difficult and painful that the help that could result from it is never engaged or experienced."[4]

> We are not the source of the truth we quietly make known, but we must be its champions. It is not enough just to listen; we must also learn to practice the skill Ephesians 4:15 calls "speaking the truth in love."

The fifth circle moves beyond mere communication to finding healthy and creative solutions to disagreements. Let's face the facts: We all *have* a problem, *live with* one, or *are* one to someone else. We are all different. We think, feel, and want very different things. Too often, our differences result in disagreements that cause untold hurt in our relationships and church communities. But we strongly believe that with God's help, it's possible to negotiate and work through our differences to solutions that will benefit the whole body. It's even possible to find healing for the unresolved hurts of the past. Of course, we will find healthy solutions to disagreements only by continuing to live out the listening lessons we have learned in all of the previous circles.

The sixth circle focuses on harmonizing our gifts and talents with the gifts of others in our communities. The New Century Version of the Bible translates Ephesians 4:16 in this way: "The whole body depends on Christ, and all the parts of the body are joined and held together. Each part does its own work to make the whole body grow and be strong with love." What a wonderful picture of cooperation.

First we have total submission to and dependence on Christ. Then we have teamwork as each member of the body uses his or her own gift in harmony with those of all the others. The miraculous result is that we grow strong together in Christ's love.

The final circle is perhaps the most exciting of all. It is the greatest miracle outcome of the miracle question so far. It is the church we've always wanted—a place where we can fully give our gifts, our talents, our dreams, and our hopes. At the same time, it is a place where we can fully receive the gifts, talents, hopes, and dreams of others. Together we all will give our best and receive God's best. We will shine like lights in the darkness, like a city on a hill that cannot be hidden. Such a church would be unstoppable and practically irresistible. This is the church transfigured and standing together with Jesus as his spotless bride. It's the walking, talking, living miracle we've all hungered for.

The big question is "Do you believe in miracles?"

ENDNOTES

1. Rick Warren, *The Purpose-Driven Church* (Grand Rapids, MI: Zondervan Publishing House, 1995), 16, 49, 128.

2. Steven de Shazer is the co-founder and Senior Research Associate at the Brief Family Therapy Center in Milwaukee, Wisconsin, and is co-developer (with Insoo Kim Berg) of the Solution-Focused Brief Therapy Model. He is the author of four groundbreaking books: *Patterns of Brief Therapy, Keys to Solutions in Brief Therapy, Clues: Investigating Solutions in Brief Therapy*, and *Putting Difference to Work* (W.W. Norton).

3. Erwin Raphael McManus, *An Unstoppable Force: Daring to Become the Church God Had in Mind* (Loveland, CO: Group Publishing, Inc., 2001), 189-190.

4. Ibid., 190.

▐▐▐ The Miracle Question ▐▐▐

Think about your church, your vision, your mission, your purpose, and your people. Then ask yourself this question:

If a miracle happened tonight and you returned to the church tomorrow with everything and everyone operating just the way God intended, what would be happening?

Be sure to dream big and think of all the unlimited possibilities!

In the space provided below, describe what you would hope to see as specifically and *visually* as possible. Write what you imagine you'd be doing, feeling, and thinking if God truly had his way. Don't leave out the feelings that you'd be experiencing or the thoughts you'd be thinking. Your answers will match your situation and your community's needs. The questions below will help you get started. Go ahead...get writing!

▐ What would people visiting your church see happening?

▐ What would the people in your church be doing?

▐ What would the congregation and guests be feeling and thinking?

▐ What transformations would be taking place before your very eyes?

▐ How would you be feeling, and what would you be doing to lead these transformations?

"I know that nothing good lives in me, that is, in my sinful nature. For I have the desire to do what is good, but I cannot carry it out" (Romans 7:18).

"Praise be to the God and Father of our Lord Jesus Christ, the Father of compassion and the God of all comfort, who comforts us in all our troubles, so that we can comfort those in any trouble with the comfort we ourselves have received from God" (2 Corinthians 1:3-4).

3

A Taste of HEAVEN?

We'd just finished presenting an intensive series of training workshops to Christian leaders and church planters who'd come from cities and villages all over India to hear us. As we evaluated this experience with a few of the workshop organizers, we asked what value they thought their people had received. Without hesitation, one of them stood up and said something we have cherished and silently repeated in our hearts ever since.

In a joyful and almost reverent tone, he said, "You've given us a taste of heaven!" To understand what he meant, you have to understand the context.

Most of our Indian students had traveled for several days just to hear us. They came on noisy, overcrowded trains and underpowered but heavily laden motor scooters. Some rode ancient bicycles.

Others had walked many dusty miles on foot. As you can imagine, we felt more than a little pressure to make the training worth their effort. And as if that pressure weren't enough, we were addressing some of the most courageous and fruitful Christian workers we'd ever encountered.

The students at this training were leaders in a movement that has planted over 20,000 churches and raised up countless indigenous church planters known as "barefoot pastors." In an environment of fierce Hindu nationalism and explosive religious violence, these amazing men and women travel from village to village in rural India, proclaiming the gospel and helping to establish new churches wherever they go.

The "barefoot pastor" name comes from the unique way they've found to multiply themselves. Once a leader establishes a church with more than twenty-five members, he selects a few of his disciples, usually ordinary villagers too poor to afford shoes, to become missionaries to the next village down the road. They walk to the next village and meet its people. Then they begin serving, sharing the story of Jesus, and praying until they have made enough converts to establish a church. When that church is ready, it sends its disciples on to the next village.

The passion, commitment, and evangelistic effectiveness of these amazing Christian leaders dwarfs just about anything we've seen anywhere else in the world. So why, you may ask, did they invite us halfway around the world to teach them about quick-to-listen leadership? Because planting a church and leading one are very different propositions.

> Planting a church and leading one are very different propositions.

Our Indian church-planting friends had seen more true miracles than you or I could imagine. But even in the midst of God's miraculous work, the day-in and day-out challenge of working together with a bunch of broken, abrasive, annoying, sinful people (just like themselves) easily deteriorated into the exact opposite of the seven circles of community we talked about in the last chapter. Just like all of us, they experienced interpersonal conflicts, moral lapses by trusted colleagues, crushing disappointments, and countless other failures that result from our human frailty.

"You've given us a taste of heaven," they said, in spite of it all. Even in the midst of difficult circumstances, these Indian leaders caught a glimpse of the transforming power of true listening. When leaders truly listen, churches become places where wounded and hurting people receive nourishment for their spirits along with healing and purpose for their lives. In the process of receiving, we also learn to recycle the love and healing we've experienced and give it away to others. The church that lives the seven circles of community becomes a kind of self-perpetuating "spiritual ecosystem" that gives us all a foretaste of what heaven must be like.

As we've shared the circles of community with groups of leaders from India to Norway, we've found that most have fondly recalled brief, cherished experiences in every circle. Perhaps you have too. Maybe it was in a small group or on a mission trip. Maybe you attended a conference where you got away from the pressures of your ministry and experienced being genuinely accepted, understood, and valued. Maybe it was when you stepped out in faith, spoke the truth in love, and saw God restore and deepen a friendship. Perhaps you can recall a seemingly miraculous time you easily accomplished great things by harmonizing your gifts with those of others. If you think back, we bet you've had at least a few tantalizing tastes of what God has in mind for his church.

But in the next breath, you'll also probably admit that these experiences are something you've had difficulty maintaining in the day-to-day work of leading your ministry. We've all tasted the invigorating air, water, and food from God's healthy spiritual ecosystem, but we're not sure if it's really possible to consistently live on these while we're here on earth. If we could, most of us would open our ears and start listening in a heartbeat.

Getting back to reality, how are we to attain that "taste of heaven" in our own fractured church settings? How do we develop and *maintain* healthy communication with our followers? To provide a picture that's a little closer to home for most of us, let's go back to our friend Richard we met in Chapter 2.

After more than fifteen years in the ministry, Richard had finally found the church he'd been dreaming of since the day he'd graduated from seminary. This vibrant and growing congregation seemed committed to reaching the community around it. They'd just completed a spacious, modern, new building that was genuinely seeker-friendly. The senior pastor was a gregarious, likeable man as well as a dynamic preacher. Best of all, he was a man who was willing to take a chance on a young pastor who wasn't quite fully recovered from the failure of his last church. Richard gladly accepted the position and looked forward to launching an ambitious small-group focus in his healthy new church. Richard reported:

> *It was almost too good to be true. When I joined the staff, I was given a budget to pursue training for myself and key volunteers in my ministry. That's when I discovered Equipping Ministries International (EMI). I'd always been drawn to relational kinds of things. And after living through the conflicted environment of my former church, I realized the potential value of equipping my small-group leaders to be good listeners. Even then, I knew that listening is the heart and soul of a good small group.*

> *I attended EMI's "Listening for Heaven's Sake" training course as a kind of bonding road trip with my team. I assumed that it would be a nice review of basic principles I'd already mastered and that it could give me a common language for communicating with my leaders. Boy, was I in for a shock! It didn't take long for me to realize that I wasn't a very good listener after all in my ministry role—or in my relationship with my wife and kids.*

> *That realization shattered the image I had of myself. I realized that I'd been passive, waiting for others to come to me so I could dispense some of my wisdom and perhaps even fix them. I began to see that the Father's heart for people is to run out to meet* them—*to love them where* they are *and not where I want them to be. That weekend I committed myself to doing whatever it took to become quick to listen. It was both fun and humbling to be learning right along with the people I was supposed to be training as leaders.*

> *Our little band of leaders quickly agreed that all of our sixty or so new group leaders should experience EMI's training as soon as possible. EMI agreed to send a training team to our church, and soon we were off and running. Our leaders were enthusiastically soaking up the training and learning how to teach it to others. It felt really good.*

> *I'd been at the church for six months, and things were going great. Some of our small groups were thriving and others were*

just getting off the ground when suddenly we all discovered that our perfect church wasn't as perfect as we had thought. The same pastor who had befriended me and given me a new lease on life and ministry was caught having an affair with a female staff member.

The "church I'd always wanted" was suddenly engulfed in a storm of hurt, betrayal, and disappointment. I was just as grieved and stunned as everyone else. Images of the bad old days I'd left behind with my previous job loomed large in my mind. Though the senior pastor and the staff member with whom he'd been inappropriately involved soon moved on, I stayed to help pick up the pieces and steer our people through an extremely difficult time of grief and healing. Though I'll admit I thought about leaving to avoid the inevitable trauma, confusion, and anger, I sensed that God had been preparing my core leaders and me for a time such as this.

Outside of divorce or the death of someone we love, there are few experiences more devastating than what was happening in Richard's new church. Their beloved and trusted senior pastor, who'd stirred the hearts of so many with a wonderful vision for knowing God and reaching their community for Christ, was gone. The infectious energy of growth they'd known only weeks before was suddenly replaced by a dull sense of disappointment, disillusionment, and distrust toward the leaders who remained. Emotions ran high, and nerves were threadbare. Families were abandoning the church as if it were a sinking ship.

Whether you live in India or Indiana, starting out healthy and staying healthy are two different things. The small tastes of heaven we've had in the seven circles of community are real, but they require constant care and energy to maintain. There are seven earthly circles of disunity and disappointment that will quickly draw us into their orbit if we let them. Let's take a closer look at those now.

Doing What Comes Naturally Stinks

In our culture, *natural* is used synonymously with *good, fresh,* and *healthy.* Natural foods are better than processed foods. Natural talent is better than skill acquired through years of hard work and struggle. Doing something naturally means doing it effortlessly, without ever breaking a sweat. Unfortunately, when it comes to living out our faith, *the only thing that comes naturally is sin.* Everything else takes work—God's work and our cooperation.

Following our normal human tendencies, relationships within our churches go through a natural process of evolution. Unfortunately, this evolution is very similar to what takes place inside our Tupperware when we leave leftovers in the refrigerator for a few weeks. They evolve naturally into something we don't even want to touch, much less eat. Likewise, in the church, our wholesome desire for growth can naturally decay into turf wars, blame shifting, and apathy. Like the rotting leftovers, the resulting state of affairs is hardly spiritually nourishing. Whether we like it or not, instead of health and harmony, our natural human tendency is to produce communities of sickness, dysfunction, and strife. Instead of being quick to listen, we are quick to give our opinions, quick to get angry, and even quicker to get even.

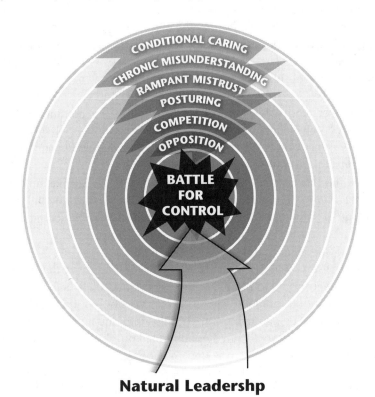

CONDITIONAL CARING
CHRONIC MISUNDERSTANDING
RAMPANT MISTRUST
POSTURING
COMPETITION
OPPOSITION
BATTLE FOR CONTROL

Natural Leadershp

Even with the best of human intentions, the seven circles of community—our "taste of heaven"—naturally devolve into disunity, chaos, and conflict. The first three earthly circles show what *naturally* takes place in every human institution, including the church. When we fail to communicate caring, understanding, and respect, outsiders feel even more alienated and stay out in record numbers. When we follow our natural human tendency to exclude anyone who doesn't look, dress, think, or behave as we do, outsiders quickly get the message that they must either conform to our culture-specific ways or face rejection. Sadly, even many insiders get this message.

Unless we learn *heavenly* ways of sharing God's acceptance, understanding, and respect with one another, we will chronically compete for control over the community's finite resources. Church staff and members will continue to gather into factions to battle over issues as large as vision and as small as the color of carpeting. As the wounds from these battles fester, they cause estrangement, misunderstanding, and disrespect. Even for many cherished family members, this community is certainly not "the safest place on earth" that Dr. Larry Crabb describes in his excellent book by the same title.[1] Instead, it is a hazardous place where acceptance must be earned and where love is precariously conditional.

Until we learn how to be real with one another, disclose our weaknesses, and speak the truth in love, all of our communication will be combative and ineffective. Even leaders who desperately want to work things out so the church can get somewhere will soon tire of the constant frustration and miscommunication.

At the heart of these circles of disunity and despair lies a never-ending *battle for control.* Leaders in these devolving communities become either pawns of influential individuals within the community or tyrants themselves. Yuck! "Doing what comes naturally" really stinks for the leaders and for everyone involved.

The seven circles of disunity highlight the bad news that causes every human institution to spiral toward eventual destruction. Sadly, Christians are not immune. Just like everyone else on the planet, our marriages struggle and fail, our friendships implode and die. Our natural human condition also creates additional problems that are unique to Christians: Our doctrinally sound churches split, and our otherwise-effective ministries melt down in bitter power struggles. It can happen to anyone, and it has happened to many who are reading this book.

Saint Augustine illustrates this bad news in a different way. In his classic work *The City of God*, he describes two cities: the eternal, incorruptible City of God and the depraved, corrupt City of Man.[2] The City of God is the source of all that is true, noble, right, pure, lovely, admirable, excellent, and praiseworthy. It is full of the miraculous healing and harmony we've pictured in the seven circles of community. Only it's more than a mere "taste of heaven." The City of God is real and solid, and it will last forever.

The City of Man, on the other hand, is full of shoddy imitations and broken promises that beguile the flesh and deceive the ego. Cheap, earthly lust stands in for priceless, God-given love. Human praise and worldly success substitute for the heavenly assurance we crave—an assurance that can only be fully satisfied by hearing our Master say, "Well done, good and faithful servant!" (Matthew 25:21).

As Christians, we live on the very boundary between God's city and man's. At times, the City of God is so close that we can almost taste it. But more often our humanity gets the best of us, and we stray toward the City of Man. Only Jesus himself avoided all the temptations of man's city, and it is his example we must look to and his voice we must listen for.

We may hunger for the City of God and long for the *heavenly* leadership outcomes we talked about in the last chapter, but in our human condition, we are naturally drawn toward the very *earthly* leading and following styles of the City of Man. In the City of Man, grand organizational schemes and corporate aspirations replace God's ideal of the church as his redeemed and blushing bride. As C.S. Lewis so eloquently put it, we are "like an ignorant child who wants to go on making mud pies in a slum because he cannot imagine what is meant by the offer of a holiday at the sea."[3]

How Do You Picture Success?

We asked the church leaders in India, "How do you think the majority of your followers might describe a successful congregation?" Their answers were not all that different from what we hear in churches in the United States.

Before we talk about what they said, let's talk about you. If you polled a random sample of church attendees, what specific signs do you think they would list to describe a successful church? Go ahead;

use the space provided on page 51 to take a stab at it. Write down at least five things you think you might hear. Better yet, ask a few random members to give you their lists.

In the United States, many, perhaps most, congregations and their leaders envision success as a collection of large, shining buildings with overflowing parking lots. We also like to imagine fabulous preaching and top-quality music and youth ministries. We dream of multimillion-dollar budgets that allow us to provide the very best programming to the widest possible audience.

In India, just having a building that keeps out the rain and provides shelter from the sun is a huge sign of success. Great preaching also made the list, along with having musical instruments and sound systems so more people could hear. Both Indians and Americans tend to paint pictures of successful churches being led by brilliant, powerful, virtuous, and nearly perfect leaders.

None of these are bad things in themselves. But how well do these signs of success line up with God's design? Do the things we hope and strive for derive from our respective human cultures or from God?

If constant cooperation and perpetually unbroken fellowship are possible anywhere on earth, I think we would have found more of them among the barefoot pastors of India. They are as courageous and committed as any group of Christians on the planet, but like yours, their churches are filled with and led by people who are all too human. Because of this, they have most of the same conflicts, ego trips, gossip problems, and all the assorted forms of unfaithfulness that churches in the United States have. But in some cases, their negative experiences are magnified because the passion of their faith and the risks they take are more intense. Betrayals and conflicts are far more devastating and painful when they involve people you've trusted with your very life.

Church planters in India and thousands of pastors and leaders like Richard have all come to the same conclusion. Their churches would be perfect if leaders were faultless and followers were totally unselfish. Even Jesus, a perfect leader if ever there was one, had days when "Get thee behind me, Satan!" was the nicest thing he could say to his top leadership trainee. The odds are that imperfect leaders like us will struggle even more.

Yet in spite of all the challenges that our Indian friends and thousands of leaders like Richard face every day, they are standing firm. Instead of denying their troubles or giving in by continuing to do what's natural, they've begun to apply *biblical solutions.* We believe God has provided us with a way to equip his people with attitudes and skills to build up and strengthen the body. We want to help the church do as Ephesians 4:12-13 teaches, "to prepare God's people for works of service, so that the body of Christ may be built up until we all reach unity in the faith and in the knowledge of the Son of God and become mature, attaining to the whole measure of the fullness of Christ." Over the last twenty-two years, we've seen God use proactive listening to help this heavenly goal become more of an earthly reality.

Think about it. How many problems that you have right now could be helped if everybody involved was a little quicker to listen, a little slower to speak, and a lot slower to get angry? Christlike listening is probably at least part of the solution to the damaged friendships, struggling marriages, conflicted ministry teams, stonewalling committee members, and the thousand other stubborn problems you may be dealing with right now.

Pastor Erwin McManus' answer to the miracle question we've posed is that he wants to see God's people become "an unstoppable force" in our culture. In his book by the same name, McManus quotes "the great sociologist" Rodney King's unforgettable question, "Can't we all just get along?" According to McManus, "The answer, of course, is no. We can't all just get along. We've proven it time and time again in history."[4] Getting along with the people inside and outside of the church will surely take a miracle.

But if, like our friends in India, you've had even a little taste of heaven, it's a lot easier to believe that God can work miracles among us. As those courageous leaders gathered from every part of their deeply divided country, they overcame regional and language differences that had separated them throughout their lives. And here's the real miracle: They found the love of Jesus Christ expressed in the flesh. They were trusted, and they trusted others enough to open their hearts. They shared with previously unthinkable honesty. They confessed their fears and failures and experienced forgiveness. They listened to God and to each other. And for a little while at least, they actually felt like beloved brothers and sisters who shared the same amazing Father. They breathed the air, tasted the water, and shared the bread of life.

There are many obstacles that prevent God's people from spending more time tasting heaven's joys and sharing them with those on earth. In the next chapter, we'll focus on understanding these impediments and finding practical solutions to overcome them. It gets a little personal, but it's more than worth it.

ENDNOTES

1. Larry Crabb, *The Safest Place on Earth: Where People Connect and Are Forever Changed* (Nashville, TN: W Publishing Group, 1999).

2. Saint Augustine, *The City of God* (New York, NY: Random House, Inc., 1950).

3. C.S. Lewis, *The Weight of Glory: and Other Addresses* (San Francisco, CA: HarperCollins, 1980), 26.

4. Erwin Raphael McManus, *An Unstoppable Force: Daring to Become the Church God Had in Mind* (Loveland, CO: Group Publishing, Inc., 2001), 53.

▋▋▋ Describe a Successful Church ▋▋▋

1. I think most people in our congregation (or ministry) would describe a successful church in the following terms...

2. To become more successful, most people in our congregation (or ministry) need to...

3. How is this list different from the one you made in the last chapter? How is it similar?

"Listening. I don't mean just hearing. Not simply smiling and nodding while somebody's mouth is moving. Not merely staying quiet until it's 'your turn' to say something. All of us are good at that game."[1]
—Charles Swindoll

4

Listening Without
A LICENSE

Mark Twain once commented, "Everybody talks about the weather, but nobody does anything about it."[2] Listening is a lot like that. Many currently available books on team building and organizational structure highlight the importance of leaders who listen, but they don't actually tell us how to do it.[3] This do-it-yourself approach to listening would work well if good listening skills came naturally. But, unfortunately, as we've discussed in previous chapters, our natural tendency is to listen too poorly, too little, and too late to make a real difference. We do the exact opposite of what James 1:19 teaches, and our organizations, churches, and families suffer as a result. The world is full of leaders who are listening without a license!

Think back to when you learned to ride a bicycle or drive a car. Your innate fears and the automatic habits you'd developed to protect yourself from falling and crashing actually fought against you. At first your brain and your muscles just weren't cooperating. Do you remember how terrifying and awkward it felt? Part of you was shouting, "Danger! Danger! Danger!" But there was another part of you that was determined to overcome the obstacles and master the skill.

If you were lucky, you had a caring parent or a more experienced friend to guide you and cheer you on. When you made mistakes or felt like giving up, that person encouraged you. He or she showed you the ropes and gave you important feedback on how to stay safe and improve your skills.

Unfortunately, when I (Dave) reached driving age, my parents were going through a difficult divorce. They were too exhausted and distracted by the crazy things that were happening in their lives to teach me how to drive. And there was no money to add me to their insurance or to pay for driver education through my school. I went as long as I could without driving. I rode my bicycle everywhere until I earned enough money to buy my own car. By then I was a college student and too embarrassed to ask anyone to teach me how to drive, so I taught myself.

Without any license or permit, I got in my car and started giving myself driving lessons. I'd watched others enough to figure out the ignition, gas pedal, and brakes. With my heart pounding in my throat, I started the car and slowly crept down back streets to a nearby stadium parking lot. When I got there, I drove in circles and practiced stopping, turning, and backing up for hours and hours. Eventually I ventured out onto the road and began driving for real. I was terrified but determined. Although I somehow managed to pass the driving test, I was a terrible driver. My wife says in my case *terrible* is a charitable description.

I understood all the basic principles and aced the written part of the driving test, but there were huge gaps in my practical understanding. Not knowing any better, I had developed many bad habits. I had trouble with left-hand turns, rarely remembered to signal before pushing my way into traffic, and drove so far to the right in two-way traffic that no passenger or mailbox was safe. It wasn't until I was nearly twenty-five that a good friend gave up a weekend to secretly reteach me how to drive.

When it comes to listening, many of us are self-taught or have learned what we know by imitating imperfect role models. Christian leaders don't instinctively know how to be quick to listen any more than teens automatically know how to drive safely. You may have watched others and figured out what to do through trial and error.

However, there are probably at least a few areas in which all of us could use some helpful feedback and even some wholesale reteaching. Even though you no doubt have lots of listening drive time under your belt, buckle up and ride along as we review two common forms of listening that can be frustrating and hazardous to everyone on the road.

Reactive Listening

There are two potentially perilous approaches to listening that Christian leaders commonly run into (no driving pun intended). The first and most widespread peril we fall into is something we call *reactive* listening. Reactive listening doesn't involve much real listening at all. In reactive listening, we hear just enough of what someone is saying to have an emotional reaction. Then we fire back an emotion-driven response. If you have ever had children (or been one), you have probably experienced how it feels to be both a perpetrator and a victim of this frustrating kind of listening. These following reactive listening exchanges might sound familiar:

Pastor: I'm a bit concerned about the giving trends I've been seeing over the past few months.
Elder: It's not our fault. They need stronger leadership and more fire in the preaching. It's time to dump all this seeker-friendly garbage and get back to proclaiming God's Word like we should've been doing all along...

Employee: Something is wrong with the photocopier.
Employer: Give me a minute, and I'll see to it. *(Muttering under her breath, "Doesn't anyone around here know how to follow simple maintenance instructions? I'm getting sick of taking care of everything myself...")*

Parent: Judy, I need to talk to you about something.
Teenager: Oh, no, here it comes, another lecture! You don't care about me; you just want to run my life! I hate you! Just leave me alone.

Wife: Honey, we need to talk...
Husband: (No reply, just the sound of tires screeching as he makes a hasty getaway.)

Reactive listening is to communication what clenched jaws and tightened fists are to a conflict. It's an early warning sign that nothing constructive is likely to come out of this exchange. For whatever reason, the reactive listener is signaling that he or she isn't really interested in what anyone else is saying. Though it isn't always as dramatic as the examples we've just given, reactive listening usually triggers a one-way monologue.

Most of us have experienced the sinking feeling that comes when we've unwittingly pulled the lever that set in motion the dumper on someone's emotional dump truck. If we had known that our words were going to unleash such a flood of anxiety, anger, or fear, we would probably never have opened our mouths. That's the effect reactive listening has on people who experience it. Parents whose teenagers go ballistic, wives whose husbands bolt at the smallest hint of a relational discussion, and leaders who've had followers unload on them all quickly learn to clam up about anything that's likely to trigger these kinds of responses. No longer expecting to be heard or understood, they begin to smooth over anything that may potentially produce anxiety.

Pretty soon, if we are still able to communicate at all, we place anything but the most innocuous topics off limits. Husbands who've experienced reactive listening from their wives know what subjects to steer clear of. Followers who've experienced it from their leaders learn to be secretive and subtly deceptive. In nearly every case, the things that are swept under the rug are usually those that most desperately need to be discussed and dealt with.

In Dave's bachelor days, he worked for a family counseling agency and spent a lot of time "shaking out" the emotional debris that troubled teens and parents had tried to sweep away. He recalls:

> *At the time I had a jampacked caseload of more than forty families, and I was expected to see each of them for an hour every week. As you can imagine, families were often stacked up in my outer office waiting to be seen. One day as I wolfed down a sandwich between sessions, I heard the receptionist sending a new family into my office. As they came in the door, I hurriedly stuffed the uneaten half of my tuna salad sandwich into the breast pocket of my sport coat and rose to greet them.*

It was a hot day, and as the session progressed, the aroma of the rapidly liquefying tuna in my pocket became increasingly stronger and more distracting. Eventually I couldn't stand it, so I casually excused myself, took off my jacket, hung it in my office closet, shut the door, and forgot all about it. Three weeks later—yes, you knew what was coming, didn't you?—I opened the closet door and was greeted by a nasty smell and a coat that now sported a growth resembling a bright green Chia Pet where the breast pocket should have been.

In those days, that was the best (in fact, the only) jacket I had. So I took it to a nearby dry cleaner and asked if there was anything they could do to save it. With a slightly disgusted shake of her head, the lady at the counter explained, "If you'd left the sandwich in there for a few hours, or even a day or two, we probably could have helped, but now the mold has eaten away the fabric."

This long-ago fashion misadventure constantly reminds me of what can happen when I avoid dealing with sticky interpersonal problems. It would be nice if they stayed safely tucked away where I left them, but they don't. They continue to evolve and take on a disgusting but flourishing life of their own. Left unaddressed, they will eventually destroy the fabric of the relationships I care about most.

Reactive listening seriously erodes trust within many relationships and organizations. If it's so clearly distasteful and obviously destructive, why do we persist in our reactive listening behaviors?

"Animal" Reactions

If you're honest with yourself, you'll probably admit that sometimes when people talk to you, instead of being quick to listen, you react by kicking into a quick-to-anger, quick-to-worry, quick-to-placate, or quick-to-run-away mode. It isn't usually a conscious decision. As you instinctively perceive some threat to the peace and tranquillity of your mental kingdom, your defenses automatically switch on.

Harvard psychologist Dr. Susan Heitler has identified four fundamental types of automatic reactions that take place when this happens.[4] Though we may react in any or all of these four ways, we usually naturally gravitate toward one particular reaction mode in our day-to-day relationships.

 The first kind of reaction is an angry or aggressive response we will compare to a *roaring lion.* Instead of listening any further, the lion in you responds aggressively. When something threatening enters your territory, arguments, accusations, sarcasm, criticism, and blame can spring unbidden to your lips. Though you're not normally a hostile person, when you're upset or caught off guard, the lion in you can wake up and roar.

To determine if this is your most frequent instinctive response, ask yourself the following questions. Would other people say

- they've seen you lose your temper or fly off the handle from time to time?
- they've had to walk on eggshells around you to avoid being snapped at?
- they've noticed you have a penchant for making cutting or sarcastic remarks?
- they've watched you fiercely defend your opinions or your territory?
- they've heard you aggressively shoot down others' suggestions or feedback?

If you answered "yes" to more than one of these questions, on good days you may be a big pussy cat (sheathing your claws), but on bad days you probably have to resist instinctively reacting in a quick-to-anger lion mode. If this beast doesn't sound like you, save your satisfied purr for later; there are three more reactive listening animals to go.

 The second typical reactive listening response is the quick-to-worry *"deer in the headlights."* Sometimes the people around you say things that push your buttons in ways that trigger intense worry and apprehension. Instead of listening further, you can become immobilized with indecision. You anticipate multiple worst-case scenarios and become unable to decide which ones to respond to. When this panic response is triggered, you can feel pulled in a hundred directions.

To determine whether this is your most frequent instinctive response, ask yourself the following questions. Would other people say

■ they've seen you drive yourself half crazy worrying?
■ they've had to be careful not to say things that might cause you to fret?
■ they've watched you lose it when things haven't gone exactly as planned?
■ they've had to talk you down from the edge of disappointment or despair?
■ they've noticed you developing headaches, stomachaches, or other physical symptoms that can be traced to high anxiety?

If you answered "yes" to more than one of these questions, you sometimes react like a deer in the headlights when you're caught off guard and not focused on listening.

 The third animal is perhaps the most common in well-mannered Christian circles. We compare the quick-to-placate reaction to a *possum* that rolls over and plays dead whenever it feels threatened by something it hears. The possum offers apparent agreement without ever asserting his or her own personal wants or needs. Surprisingly, the possum reaction is probably one of the greatest sources of hurt and anger that we see in churches. People who chronically give up and give in without thinking are often chronically unhappy. They often feel like hopeless victims of an unjust system in which the cards are stacked against them.

To determine whether this is your most frequent instinctive response, ask yourself the following questions. Would other people say

■ they've been concerned that you are too nice for your own good?
■ they've noticed that you rarely stand up for yourself or ask for help?
■ they've observed that you're very careful never to make waves?
■ they've seen you go far out of your way to avoid possible unpleasantness?
■ they've watched others exploit your generosity and unselfishness?

If you answered "yes" to more than one of these questions, sometimes you tend to instinctively react like a possum.

The fourth reactive listening response is the quick-to-run-away *rabbit*. When the rabbit hears something unsettling, he or she disappears quickly into the underbrush. You might change the subject, physically leave the room, or mentally check out to a happy place where others can't reach you.

According to Dr. Heitler, when people who react this way run away *from* something, they usually run *to* something else. Generally speaking, this means running from deeper human connections to find substitutes elsewhere, making the runner susceptible to compulsive behaviors such as overwork, overindulgence in food or television, or a wide variety of other potential addictions.

To determine whether this is your most frequent instinctive response, ask yourself the following questions. Would other people say

- they've sometimes experienced you as aloof or emotionally unavailable?
- they've noticed that you don't like to talk about serious matters?
- they've seen you make excuses to evade people you don't wish to see?
- they've thought that when things get tough, you get going—somewhere else?
- they've observed that it's hard to pin you down?

If you answered "yes" to more than one of these questions, your automatic reactions may fit the rabbit's profile.

Now delve a little more deeply into this subject by completing the work sheet on page 64.

If you don't like any of the animals we've been describing, you're not alone. Reactivity is rarely pleasant, but it is part of being human. Each of the animal reactions we've discussed represents a natural defensive reaction that is hard-wired into your brain. Every reaction is there for a purpose: to help you survive on your own in hostile environments. However, these natural reactions work against us in situations that require mutual cooperation and teamwork. Just like the old instincts that got in the way of learning to ride a bike or drive a car, these natural defensive reactions have to be tamed if we wish to effectively serve and lead others.

When we allow these defensive beasts to run loose, they can sabotage our personal and leadership goals in these ways: the lion with rage, the deer with anxiety, the possum with codependency, and the rabbit with aloofness. You may have already experienced the chaos and alienation each of these inner beasties can create. When animals begin fighting and devouring one another, it's not a pretty sight. So how can we stop the carnage and learn to be quick to listen instead of quick to react? Before we can answer that, we need to look at a slightly less destructive approach we'll call passive listening.

Passive Listening

When most people hear the word *listen*, they're thinking of passive listening. We call it *passive listening* because mostly it involves *not* doing something—not talking mostly. Passive "listening" is what most people do in church during the sermon, but is it really listening? Someone else is talking, and we're not, so we're listening, right? OK, not always, and often not very well. Just ask the people you meet after church to give you the main points of the message their minister has worked all week to prepare. You will find some who can repeat each point with great clarity and many more who can't. That's because one-way communication is much less memorable than conversations in which we actually participate actively.

> Silence may be the beginning of wisdom, and it may indeed be golden, but it's not really the same as listening.

So what's wrong with passive listening? Proverbs 17:28 tells us, "Even a fool is thought wise if he keeps silent, and discerning if he holds his tongue." On a similar note, Proverbs 21:23 says, "He who guards his mouth and his tongue keeps himself from calamity." Silence may be the beginning of wisdom, and it may indeed be golden, but it's not really the same as listening.

Most of the time, keeping your mouth shut is far better and wiser than allowing the instinctive animal reactions we spoke of earlier to take over. But true listening requires that we concentrate on understanding what someone is saying rather than just passively taking it in. Listening is much more than the lack of talking. Perhaps that's why in Hebrew, Greek, and English, the verb *listen* has a threefold meaning.

It simultaneously includes the ideas of hearing, understanding, and acting on what's being said.

Perhaps the most famous biblical command to appear in both the Old and New Testaments is recorded in Deuteronomy 6:4-5 and Mark 12:29-30. It reads, "Hear, O Israel: The Lord our God, the Lord is one. Love the Lord your God with all your heart and with all your soul and with all your strength." In the original Hebrew, in the Greek translation of Christ's words, and in any decent English translation, the intent is the same. When we read, "Hear, O Israel," we realize that the Israelites are being asked to do more than merely listen to the words as if they were lyrics to some popular new tune. They are being directed to ponder them in their hearts and then act in new ways because of what they've understood. This is a divine summons and a holy calling to focus their whole beings into living differently from what comes naturally for them.

James 1:19 issues a similar call to all Christians. "Be quick to listen" is not something to which we are to passively assent or to smile and say, "It sure would be nice if everybody listened like that." It's an active and unconditional command. Obedient Christians who read these words can't be passive about how they connect with God or other people. For in addition to "loving the Lord our God," Jesus goes on to command us to love our neighbors as we want to be loved ourselves (Mark 12:31). In order to satisfy our own deep longing to be heard, then, we need to equip ourselves to truly listen to others.

Yes, passive listening is a little bit better than reactive listening because at least our neighbor gets to talk. But it doesn't communicate much love or concern. For one thing, people can't tell whether we're actually listening or replaying last night's football game in our heads. This is why countless wives complain of the passivity of their husbands. "I can't tell if he hears me and cares what I'm talking about or not." However, we've seen lots of men *and women* who've mastered the art of hiding any sign that might indicate that they are paying attention. Instead of showing transparent interest, they've learned to play games that give them a sense of power and keep their partners guessing about where they really stand. We can say without much fear of contradiction that this is not how most people like to be loved.

When people listen in ways that show they're attentive and involved in what we're saying, we feel accepted, understood, and valued. When they don't, we fill in the blanks and assume that they are indifferent and that we're insignificant in their eyes. Even if they do care, we aren't able to tell because a very important piece of the communication puzzle is missing.

Interestingly enough, this passivity can actually create hostility or reactivity. When we encounter passive listeners (especially the natural lions among us), we keep "bumping up the volume" until we get a satisfactory response. If you've ever been a tourist at Buckingham Palace, you've seen this dynamic in action. The Buckingham Palace guards are famous for their stoic impassivity. They've been trained to stand very still, stare straight ahead, and ignore the hundreds of tourists who've come to take pictures of them. Getting the guards to react is a challenge most tourists can't resist. Nice people who wouldn't ordinarily bother or offend anyone can't seem to help making goofy faces and explosively rude noises. They will do almost anything to get a response.

> The more passive we act, the more the people around us tend to get anxious and act out.

We all crave feedback, and when we don't get enough of it, we start acting weird. The more passive we act, the more the people around us tend to get anxious and act out. When your kids, your church members, or your staff people don't receive the affirmation and feedback they crave, they can also begin to act out. Not consciously at first, but consistently and predictably. Often when we find leaders' families and congregations in crisis, we can trace the origins of heartbreaking problems back to passive communication styles.

Sooner or later, two-way *active* communication needs to happen. And sooner is almost always better than later. The wise leader knows that, as the old saying goes, "an ounce of prevention is better than a mountain of excuses." OK, that's not how the saying goes, but it's true nonetheless. If we want to be effective in our mission to love the world into relationship with Jesus, we have to learn better ways to listen and cooperate. We can't just keep on being passive and reactive. To experience the circles of caring community, we have to learn how to become active and proactive listeners.

In the next chapter, we'll focus on learning to move beyond our natural, unhealthy tendencies into intentional, *premeditated acts of listening.*

ENDNOTES

1. Charles Swindoll, *Growing Strong in the Seasons of Life* (Grand Rapids, MI: Zondervan Publishing House, 1983), 69.

2. John Bartlett, *Familiar Quotations: A Collection of Passages, Phrases, and Proverbs Traced to Their Sources in Ancient and Modern Literature* (New York, NY: Little, Brown & Company, 1992), 528.

3. Many secular and Christian books recommend using effective listening skills in leading. They include Stephen R. Covey, *The Seven Habits of Highly Effective People: Restoring the Character Ethic* (New York, NY: Fireside, 1990); Stephen R. Covey, *Principle-Centered Leadership* (New York, NY: Fireside, 1992); Daniel Goleman, *Emotional Intelligence* (New York, NY: Bantam Books, 1995); Laurie Beth Jones, *Jesus, CEO: Using Ancient Wisdom for Visionary Leadership* (New York, NY: Hyperion, 1995); John C. Maxwell, *Attitude 101: What Every Leader Needs to Know* (Nashville, TN: Thomas Nelson Publishers, 2003); John C. Maxwell, *Equipping 101* (Nashville, TN: Thomas Nelson Publishers, 2003); Andy Stanley, *The Next Generation Leader: 5 Essentials for Those Who Will Shape the Future* (Sisters, OR: Multnomah Publishers, 2003).

4. Susan Heitler, *From Conflict to Resolution: Strategies for Diagnosis and Treatment of Distressed Individuals, Couples, and Families* (New York, NY: W.W. Norton and Company, 1990), 59-63.

▌▌▌ Animal Reactions ▌▌▌

Based on what you've been reading, do you think you tend to react more like…

a lion?	a deer in the headlights?	a possum?	a rabbit?

1. How do you think this affects your relationships?

2. How do you think it affects the people you lead?

"I keep asking that the God of our Lord Jesus Christ, the glorious Father, may give you the Spirit of wisdom and revelation, so that you may know him better. I pray also that the eyes of your heart may be enlightened in order that you may know the hope to which he has called you, the riches of his glorious inheritance in the saints, and his incomparably great power for us who believe" (Ephesians 1:17-19a).

5

Opening the Eyes (and Ears) OF YOUR HEART

Most of the leaders who take our courses or read our books have had some exposure to secular "active listening" training. Somewhere along the way, they've been taught how to use basic verbal formulas that actively test their understanding. Most know how to use phrases such as "It sounds like you feel so-and-so" or to ask, "Am I hearing you say such and such?"

Though its origins are in modern psychology[1] and not Scripture, active listening is healthier and more compatible with Christ's compassion than any of the listening approaches we've previously discussed. Though some may say they have issues with using any method or tool that isn't specifically mentioned in the Scriptures, many faithful men and women have transformed secular tools to serve God's ends. Martin Luther reworded popular drinking songs and turned them into powerful hymns that have inspired God's people for centuries. Billy Graham has used television (some would say a devil's tool if ever there was one) to bring millions to Jesus. In the same way, such brilliant Christian counselors as Paul Tournier,[2] Gary Collins,[3] Larry Crabb,[4] Paul Meier,[5] Rich Walters,[6] and Gary Sweeten[7] have redirected the tools of psychology and active listening to serve God's purposes and to help countless thousands of people experience abundant Christian living.

> We temporarily set aside our personal agendas and open the eyes and ears of our hearts so that we may serve another person.

Even if active listening is imperfect, it gives the people we're talking with feedback, room to talk, and a sense that we might possibly care enough to try to understand them. Active listening is not just a tool for counselors or pastors; it's something anybody who cares about people can master and harness for God's purposes. It's a tool every teacher, small group leader, pastor, elder, deacon, parent, student, friend, and neighbor can master—if we are willing to die to ourselves.

There are three essential elements to what we will call *Christlike* active listening: (1) communicating genuine caring, (2) communicating authentic understanding, and (3) communicating Christlike respect. In these three ways, we temporarily set aside our personal agendas and open the eyes and ears of our hearts so that we may serve another person.

When Jesus told the disciples in Matthew 26:41 and Mark 14:38 that their spirits may have been willing but their flesh was too weak, he was pointing out a difficult truth. When it comes to self-sacrifice, good intentions alone won't do the job. As Peter the apostle could testify from his real-life experience, talking about laying down your life for someone and actually doing it are two very different things. So how do we actually do it?

Communicating Caring

Communicating genuine caring means putting aside selfish concerns and putting your whole body to work serving someone else. Yes, we said "your body." We're talking about "full-bodied" caring here. Just as a full-bodied wine engages our senses of sight, taste, and smell with its savory richness, full-bodied caring involves your eyes, your expression, your posture, and your physical closeness and warmth. Before the first word leaves your mouth, people have already taken in a hundred little signs that tell them whether you are interested and care about them or this exchange will be business as usual.

When full-bodied, sacrificial caring is demonstrated, the other person feels a subtle but wonderful sense of acceptance. We think it may be akin to the marvelous "aroma of Christ" Paul talks about in 2 Corinthians 2:15.

On the other hand, there are also many subtle signals that betray us when our attention isn't focused on caring for the person in front of us. An impatient glance at a watch or a memo, a subtle frown pulling at the corners of your mouth, arms crossed in a defensive stance, or an unenthusiastic shading to your voice can quickly indicate that your center of attention is elsewhere.

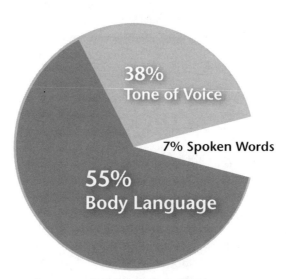

**Communication Is Much More
Than Words**

According to UCLA researcher Dr. Albert Mehrabian, our non-verbal body language and voice tone are far more significant and our words far less significant to good communication than most people imagine.[8] When there is inconsistency among the verbal message, voice tone, and nonverbal signals we're sending, listeners give far more weight to the nonverbal and voice-tone clues than to words. Body language is the most significant factor at 55 percent, followed by tone of voice at 38 percent and spoken words at a mere 7 percent. If we want to communicate caring, we have to consciously school our bodies to cooperate in the process. No matter how carefully you choose your words, your nonverbal signals will give away the truth if you lack a real investment of caring.

So how *do* we go about focusing our full attention and our whole bodies to set the stage for the ministry of listening? It all begins with an attitude. In simple terms, to communicate caring, we have to *want* to care. Notice we didn't say you have to care already; you just have to want to.

In almost every way, it's easier by far not to care, but it's not the law of Christ. Nine times out of ten, we don't feel like expending the energy or risking the potential heartaches that genuine caring entails. That doesn't mean we don't ultimately want to care, but there is usually an inner conflict in which we must choose to obey either the natural law of our flesh or Christ's law of love. If Christ wins, we have to give our schedules over to Jesus and say, "Lord, let me communicate your caring this day or during this meeting or in this conversation. I can't do it by myself." We've all had this conversation with God.

> To communicate caring, we have to *want* to care.

Jesus' chosen word for his promised presence in the Holy Spirit is *Paraclete*—"the one called alongside." When you're on top of the world, Jesus is with you. In your lowest depression, regardless of how you feel, Jesus is with you. As you struggle to overcome what comes naturally so you can truly listen, Jesus is with you!

If you want to be quick to listen, begin by engraving Jesus' promise on your mind and heart. With his help, you can do this. Philippians 2:12-13 talks about "working out" our salvation with fear and trembling because God is working inside of us "to will and to act according to his good purpose." We take this to mean that when we surrender to God's purposes, God helps our will, our wishes, and our desires become more like his. God also empowers our actions.

This is the secret of truly gracious leaders who give their complete attention to the person God has presented to them in the moment. Their time might be precious and limited, but they hold their calls, and for that moment, to them you are the most important person on planet Earth. You feel welcomed, at ease, and ready to share your heart. In these modest encounters, Christ himself seems palpably real, present, and active right there with you. If you've ever received this kind of care from a servant leader, you know how powerful and genuine it feels.

Leaders like this yield not only their hearts to God but also their bodies "as a living sacrifice" to *show* us genuine caring. As Colossians 3:12 puts it, they "clothe" themselves with the physical manifestations of "compassion, kindness, humility, gentleness and patience." What are those manifestations? Think about it, and a list of caring behaviors will probably come readily to mind.

A warm smile says, "Welcome!"

Gentle eye contact says, "I am here for you."

Leaning forward slightly says, "I'm interested."

An open posture says, "I'm open to hearing what you have to say."

Wholehearted patience says, "Take your time; you're worth it."

You may not think of mastering your body language as a significant act of service until you try it. At first it may feel foreign and unnatural because it is not "of the flesh" but an outward expression of the Spirit's fruit of love, joy, peace, patience, kindness, goodness, faithfulness, gentleness, and self-control. Temptations will abound. Fleeting ideas and anxieties will try to draw your attention away. If God has something special in mind, there will often be things happening outside your window, noises, and all manner of other distractions working against you. Your perseverance and patience will be tested, but as Hebrews 10:36 says, it will be worth it when you see the results God has in mind.

Communicating Understanding

Once you've prepared your mind and body for the ministry of connecting with others, you're ready to begin practicing the second major component of Christlike active listening. This is the work of communicating authentic understanding. Ironically, this requires realizing something that those of us who like to appear competent hate to admit: *We don't really understand what others are thinking and feeling.* This is important. We may think we understand, but unless we've been granted psychic powers, without listening we can't authentically comprehend what's happening inside someone else's heart or mind. Without taking ample time to hear people out, we are just jumping to conclusions and disrespectfully projecting our expectations on them. Anne cites an example that happened to some women from her church.

> *A recently widowed older woman we'll call Lisa shocked a well-intentioned group of ladies from our church who'd come bearing food and offering consolation after her husband's death. One of the ladies who'd lost her own husband a few years back hugged Lisa and tearfully said, "I'm so sorry. I know just how you feel."*

> *At that instant, something inside Lisa snapped. Shaking off the proffered hug, she shouted, "No, you don't! I'm not sad at all. I'm glad he's dead!" The openly shaken church ladies collapsed into chairs as Lisa poured out a heartbreaking tale of her dead husband's nearly daily acts of cruelty and abuse.*

It's tempting to project our experiences onto others, especially when we want to appear understanding and sympathetic. It's also natural to prejudge others according to our own ways of seeing things, but this clouds understanding instead of clarifying it. Anne's story illustrates that the ministry we expect to give may be poles apart from the ministry that people really need from us. Authentic understanding comes only through making the *invisible* world of someone else's motivations, thoughts, and feelings *visible* to the eyes of our own understanding. To use the words of Paul's prayer for the Ephesians, "the eyes of our heart" must be opened.

> Authentic understanding comes only through making the *invisible* world of someone else's motivations, thoughts, and feelings *visible* to the eyes of our own understanding.

▌▌▌ Emotional Ultrasound

It may sound odd, but when it comes to seeing into another person's inner life, our ears must serve as the "eyes of our heart." We have to learn to *see with our ears.* We're not trying to be mystical or poetic here; this is a profound and practical truth. It's the same principle that allows ultrasound to reveal the hidden intricacies of unborn babies without harming either mother or child. The ultrasound probe sends out gentle pulses of sound that radiate through the flesh and then reflect back differently depending on the densities of the fluids or solids they encounter. The miracle of ultrasound is in the  computer that allows it to "see" by interpreting the sound waves. That's exactly how Christlike active listening works.

Good listeners tune in to what a person says and then reflect it back in order to determine if the "picture" they are getting is accurate. Periodically they prompt the person to whom they're listening in order to confirm or clarify whether they are "seeing" what he or she means. The effort to understand demonstrates caring. It sounds very simple in theory, but doing it well takes practice and perseverance. It's a capacity that every leader will benefit from mastering. If you and those who work with you become proficient at it, your ministry and personal effectiveness will improve dramatically.

There are three essential elements that allow you to test your understanding of what is going on inside another person: identifying feelings, identifying thoughts, and tentatively reflecting thoughts and feelings, FTT for short.

■■■ Identifying Feelings

The first kind of information we want to identify is *feelings*. The question we have to ask ourselves is "What is the emotional content of the speaker's words and body language?" You'd think answering this question would be pretty simple, but many leaders struggle with a basic learning disability in this area. They confuse ideas with emotions.

It's common to hear people say things like "I feel that the church has become too commercialized" or "I feel that the best course of action is to just wait and see." Neither of these statements reflects an emotion. They are judgments or conclusions about ideas. Usually any statement that begins with "I feel that…" is describing a judgment and not a feeling. On the other hand, when people say they are feeling happy, upset, afraid, lonely, or regretful, they *are* describing emotional feelings.

In the following exercise, determine if the word *feel* is truly a feeling or if it is a thought or belief. If it is a feeling, then identify what the feeling is.

■■■ Feelings or Thoughts?

She *feels* irritated when her children will not obey her.

He *feels* that she is too strict with the children.

George *feels* like the company is not keeping its promises to him.

Mary *feels* encouraged by the good reports her boss has given her.

Some people *feel* that the leaders are not sensitive to the needs of the people.

The pastor *felt* disrespected by the negative comments from the committee.

Our elders *feel* that they should be able to make good decisions about the church.

The star basketball player *felt* overwhelmed by the pressure to win.

The boss *feels* that his vice president is *feeling* dissatisfied.

Most people *feel* apprehensive when they are placed in a new culture.

> Understanding emotion is the single most potent key to another person's inner world. If there is one listening element you don't ever want to ignore, this is it.

Another problem many people have with identifying feelings is that they have limited emotional vocabularies. Women in our classes often joke that their husbands are like cavemen who know only two feeling words: "I feel good!" and "I feel bad!" On a good day, it might be "I feel really good!" or "I feel really bad!" Sadly, although they've made a joke of it, these same women will often admit to feeling deeply frustrated and misunderstood by husbands and bosses who can't communicate about feelings. This is not just a male/female dynamic. There are many families and even whole cultures that tend to ignore or discount feelings. This is tragic when you consider that understanding emotion is the single most potent key to another person's inner world. If there is one listening element you don't ever want to ignore, this is it.

Some of us struggle with finding an appropriate feeling word to express ourselves more accurately, but not nearly as much as Anne's friend Natasha. She is from the Ukraine and came to one of our listening classes. She had come to the United States to study at Cincinnati Bible College and, after hearing about our courses, wanted to be a participant. Everything was going fine, and she understood the English quite effectively, until we formed small groups to start practicing. Anne glanced over to the small group that Natasha was a part of and noticed she was crying. Natasha then began to share with her group that she had felt all the feelings that were being described but, because of the oppression she had endured during her upbringing, she was never allowed to express any of them and really never even had the words to express them. For the first time in her life, her feelings were being validated, and she was given the freedom to feel.

Over the years we've developed our own feeling words list and used it to help leaders increase their ability to connect with others by expanding their emotional vocabularies. Without getting too crazy or detailed about it, we say all emotions fall into six basic categories: Glad, Mad, Sad, Afraid, Confused, and Ashamed. There are different shadings and intensities to each of these feelings. We might describe someone who is a little bit glad as "comfortable" or "at ease." Someone who is exceedingly glad might be "ecstatic" or "in seventh heaven." See a more complete list of words describing feelings on page 86.

> Motivation comes from emotion. Understand a person's emotions, and very soon you will have the key that energizes him or her into action.

When we listen, it's very important to tune in to the category and intensity of the feeling the person is expressing—both verbally and nonverbally. Sometimes it helps to follow along and mentally say, "It sounds like he or she is feeling such and such." Silently fill in the feeling word that most accurately expresses the emotion you are picking up from moment to moment. During any given conversation, you will start to hear and see different emotions and multiple shadings.

Leaders who make the mistake of overlooking the importance of emotion are usually the same ones who complain of poor productivity, low morale, and disloyalty among those they lead. Motivation comes from emotion. Understand a person's emotions, and very soon you will have the key that energizes him or her into action. Even those who rarely articulate feelings are moved and influenced by them. Feelings are the foundation of any passion. See if you can identify the general feeling categories and specific emotional shadings communicated in each of the following sentences. You can use the list on page 86 as a cheat sheet if you'd like.

1. I'm really ticked off at Josh. He's late again!

2. I have incredible news; you're not going to believe this!

3. I'm pretty stressed out about making this deadline.

4. I can't face Sarah after how I treated her yesterday.

5. I miss my old friends. Nobody around here really knows me.

6. I don't know where this relationship is headed.

In each case there are multiple shading possibilities, but the general feeling categories are

1. General category = Mad

Specific shadings = annoyed, fed up, or disgusted

2. General category = Glad

Specific shadings = excited, eager, or wound up

3. General category = Afraid

Specific shadings = anxious, worried, or apprehensive

4. General category = Ashamed

Specific shadings = sorry, remorseful, or self-conscious

5. General category = Sad

Specific shadings = lonesome, disconnected, or lost

6. General category = Confused

Specific shadings = perplexed, bewildered, or puzzled

You may have noticed that several of these examples don't specifically mention feeling words. But the feelings are there nonetheless. Depending on the tone of voice and body language that accompany the words, the statements could have different meanings. How can you know which is correct? Listen carefully to the person's whole communication, not just the words, and then offer your best attempt at labeling what you understand. Most people will happily correct or fine-tune any reasonable interpretation you offer. Since the goal is to show that you are *trying* to understand, close enough is usually more than good enough.

■■ Identifying Thoughts

The ability to accurately identify and understand what another person is *feeling* is the first initial in our FTT recipe for communicating authentic understanding. The second letter, *T*, stands for identifying the essential *thoughts* that are driving the person's emotional response.

To understand someone's inner world, we need to realize that people feel the way they feel because of what they are thinking. For example, think about how you feel when an expensive sports car cuts you off in traffic. Now think about how you feel when a speeding police car does the same thing. What about an ambulance? With the ambulance, we might feel pity for the injured person inside who's being rushed to the hospital. With the police car, we might feel fear because we think we are about to be pulled over. With the sports car, we're likely to boil with rage at that jerk in the expensive car. In all three cases, our feelings flow from the lightning-fast judgments we've reached in our thinking. Our brains carry out complex deliberations about how to react in milliseconds. So fast, in fact, that we usually have no conscious awareness we've made up our minds at all.

Christlike active listening helps people examine the connections between what they really think and feel. It provides a kind of reality check. So how do we identify the thoughts?

Once you have identified the feeling, it's usually a matter of connecting the dots. When a person feels happy, there is usually a reason. In your mind, you ask yourself, "Why is he or she feeling happy?" You don't usually have to be Sigmund Freud and dig deep into his or her unconscious motivations—most people will tell you without even being asked. Let's take another look at the sentences we used earlier to identify emotions. This time we will try to see if we can locate the basic thoughts that are driving the feelings in each case.

Fill in the blanks with the thoughts behind the feelings, as we've done in the first example.

1. I'm really ticked off at Josh. He's late again!
   Speaker is angry because Josh is late again.
2. I have incredible news; you're not going to believe this!
   Speaker is _____ *because* _____.
                 [feeling]   *[thought]*
3. I'm pretty stressed out about making this deadline.
   Speaker is _____ *because* _____.
                 [feeling]   *[thought]*
4. I can't face Sarah after how I treated her yesterday.
   Speaker is _____ *because* _____.
                 [feeling]   *[thought]*
5. I miss my old friends. Nobody around here really knows me.
   Speaker is _____ *because* _____.
                 [feeling]   *[thought]*
6. I don't know where this relationship is headed.
   Speaker is _____ *because* _____.
                 [feeling]   *[thought]*

In each case there may be other possibilities, but the most apparent thought-feeling connections are

1. Angry because Josh is late again.

2. Excited because she has unbelievable news.

3. Apprehensive because of the impending deadline.

4. Remorseful because of the way she's behaved toward Sarah.

5. Sad because he misses being with his friends.

6. Confused because she can't figure out the direction the relationship is taking.

Depending on how we're wired, identifying thoughts may be easier and more natural than identifying feelings, or the other way around. If leaders want to communicate authentic empathy that opens doors to real understanding, it's very important to balance the two. Too much focus on the thought side usually stems from a *need to be right*. Missing or underestimating the importance of feelings can lead to coldhearted analysis, criticism, and judgment that close down communication. The tendency to overbalance toward feelings or ignore thoughts usually stems from a *need to be liked or needed*. When this happens, we can get so lost in identifying sympathetically with a person that we become codependent as we attempt to rescue him or her.

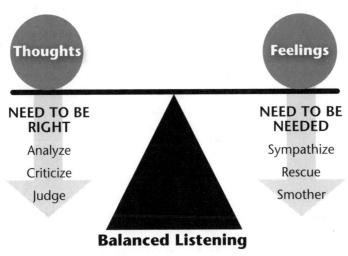

Balanced Listening

Balance is better and much healthier, especially for leaders. We will talk more about the challenges leaders with different temperaments face in keeping their listening balance in Chapters 9 and 10. Now, however, it's time to move on to the final initial in our FTT listening approach.

▋▋▋ Tentatively Reflecting Thoughts and Feelings

The third and, for most of our students, the most challenging aspect of communicating authentic understanding is *tentatively reflecting* thoughts and feelings in a brief empathic statement.

Why tentatively? We alluded to this earlier, but because it's so important, we'll say it again. Even if you are trying your best to tune in to someone else's thoughts and feelings, you can't know for certain that you're on target. Often the people we're listening to won't even know until they hear it themselves. Being tentative respectfully acknowledges that the person we're listening to is the only true expert. It also helps prevent the speaker from assuming that my tentative reflection must be the truth. Especially for a struggling or troubled follower, it's all too easy to assume that the strong leader must be right in his or her interpretation. You may be right; you may be wrong—by being tentative, you let the listener decide which it is.

Once as I (Anne) was teaching the FTT listening formula, a pastor in the class spoke up. He said, "I can do great with the feelings and thoughts, but where I really get stuck is with being tentative. It just seems wishy-washy to me, like I really don't know what I am talking about."

> You may be right; you may be wrong—by being tentative, you let the listener decide which it is.

As I listened, I realized that appearing competent was a very important characteristic to this pastor. The thought of not appearing competent to the other person felt threatening to him. The more we conversed, the more he understood that the issue was not his competency but his humility. In order for him to listen competently, he needed to humbly admit that without listening, he couldn't know for sure how another person felt or what the person believed. He was satisfied with this explanation and was able to use the skills very effectively in the class role-play situations.

Like any acquired skill, tentatively reflecting thoughts and feelings feels somewhat awkward and mechanical at first, and this is hard for the perfectionists among us. We hold fast to the credo "Anything that's worth doing is worth doing well." While this may be true, it's not the same as "Anything worth doing is worth doing perfectly and naturally the first time." As leaders, we know things don't usually work this way. Rather, we know that anything worth doing will take time to master. Like anything else, listening is worth doing inadequately at first, then doing it over and over until you begin to improve. And like learning to ride a bike or drive a car, the first few times are the most uncomfortable. Eventually we begin to develop listening reflexes and a knack for constructing empathic statements, and listening becomes more natural.

Like any new skill, listening is one that takes a lot of practice. We've been working at it for over twenty years and still sometimes catch ourselves reacting rather than responding appropriately. So as we teach leaders to listen, we break the skills down into digestible parts. Rather than progressing straight to real-life listening situations—in which leaders have a tendency to get so caught up in the situations that they immediately fall back into their old, ineffective listening patterns—we have tried to go step by step in the skill development process.

After practicing "in the parking lot" with the following mirroring and summarizing exercises, you will be ready to move out into the traffic flow of natural conversations where you can practice being even quicker to listen and slower to speak. Being quick to listen doesn't mean we've taken a vow of silence. But when others are seeking understanding, involvement, or emotional support, the quick-to-listen leader is able to keep the spotlight of care and concern on them as much as possible.

Mirroring

What do we expect to happen when we look in a mirror? We expect to see an accurate reflection of ourselves. Why? So we can decide whether we want to make any changes in our appearance to look our best. As effective listeners, it's our job to mirror the people we listen to. We are there to give an accurate reflection that will help them understand how they look and decide whether that is the way they want to stay. Consider the following examples.

Speaker: I had such an exhausting day yesterday.
Mirror: It seems like yesterday was a pretty full day for you and you're worn out.

Speaker: I don't believe I will ever finish all this homework.
Mirror: Wow, so having all this work to do is a bit overwhelming?

Speaker: My children will never do what I say.
Mirror: It sounds like your kids are frustrating the living daylights out of you.

Speaker: My boss is impossible to please.
Mirror: So trying to figure out what she wants is incredibly confusing?

Speaker: I can't believe that my wife will never try anything new.
Mirror: You're getting really impatient with your wife's fearfulness, aren't you?

Christlike active listening helps us connect with our conversational partners, but it also helps them understand themselves better. As we mirror, it's important that we creatively respond with words that accurately describe the feelings and thoughts we believe the speaker has communicated. Remember that we are trying to understand, and if we are not exactly correct in our responses, we trust that our partners will provide clarification.

Summarizing

Often a person who wants to be heard comes ready to dump an entire frustrating or exciting situation in your lap. As the listener, your challenge is to *summarize* all the information about the situation and respond in a way that connects appropriately with the speaker. You might feel the need to respond in kind with a lengthy, detailed analysis of what you've just heard. But that's probably not necessary and may not be helpful. Many times it's more effective to offer a short, tentative sentence that summarizes your perception of the speaker's feeling and thought. We like to think of summarizing as offering back a "Reader's Digest condensed version."

For example, what if, instead of simply reporting, "I had such an exhausting day yesterday," a speaker continues with the story and says, "I cleaned out my garage and could not believe all the stuff that I had accumulated. I was really rather embarrassed and mad at myself that I had let things get so out of control. I guess I am paying for it now with being so worn out. I will never let that happen again."

This story contains too many details to simply mirror back. It's time to summarize. Think about everything the speaker has said, then identify one or two key feelings and thoughts. Remember to offer your summary tentatively.

Summarize: You sound relieved to have tackled that big job, but you're paying for it physically today.

Like mirroring, summarizing will take some practice. Find a friend or co-worker to practice these techniques with you. Ask your partner to tell you which responses worked, which ones didn't, and why. Then move on to a normal conversation using three or four good empathic responses and see what happens.

When to Use Christlike Active Listening and When Not To

Although Christlike active listening can vastly improve communication and understanding in many situations, it's not always called for. If people are just looking for information, they won't thank you for trying to tune into their deep inner lives by saying something like "It sounds like you're extremely anxious to find the restroom!" If people are seeking information and you have it, give it to them so they won't burst their bladders trying to explain themselves. If you don't know, say so, and if possible refer them to someone who does. Information-seekers don't need active listening, Christlike or otherwise.

Another time active listening isn't usually helpful is when someone wants to gossip or spread rumors. In these cases, affirm the person's nobler motives as best you can, while declining to enter into that conversation. Say something like "I can tell this is important to you, but I don't feel comfortable talking about it." If the person asks why, give a direct answer, such as "I am not OK with talking about her in her absence."

Sometimes as you listen, you may feel you're getting mixed messages and you don't know for sure what the speaker is looking for. In these situations, we may be tempted to draw the spotlight back to ourselves. We do this by asking too many questions and subconsciously leading the conversation in the direction we want it to go.

This is not quick-to-listen leading at all. If anything, it's probably manipulation. Think of it in terms of taking over the steering wheel from someone in mid-drive. In these situations, we advise you to err on the side of actively listening. Instead of imposing your own perceived need, use active listening to clarify the need the speaker is trying (albeit imperfectly) to address. Truly effective leaders listen in order to discern where others want to go and to help them discover for themselves how to get there. This idea brings us to the third major component of Christlike active listening, the topic of communicating Christlike respect.

Communicating Respect

Fill in the blank. Respect must be _____. If you said "earned," you are accurately stating the majority opinion. In this case, though, the majority view is at odds with biblical teaching. The world's belief regarding respect is that *our worth comes from our works.* Nothing could be further from the truth.

According to Genesis 1:27, every human being on planet Earth is created in God's image. Romans 5:18 and other teachings throughout the New Testament proclaim that every person's worth is irrevocably established by Christ's sacrifice. None of us earned it or had anything to do with it. Perhaps that's why 1 Peter 2:17 orders Christians to "show proper respect to everyone." This doesn't apply just to the wealthy or accomplished, the intelligent or attractive. It doesn't apply just to other Christians or to those with whom we agree; "everyone" means *everyone.*

So what does this have to do with listening? The answer is *everything.* We take time to listen to the people we respect. We treat them as equals and not inferiors. We don't try to fool those we respect, manipulate them, or take advantage of them to get what we want or make ourselves look good. We let them face their own responsibilities and make their own decisions.

Jesus modeled this kind of respect in the way he treated the rich, young ruler who asked him how to gain eternal life (Matthew 19:16-22). When the young man decided the cost Jesus required was too high, "he went away sad, because he had great wealth." And Jesus didn't try to stop him. He didn't try to bargain with him, lecture him, or frighten him into submission. It must have been heartbreakingly painful for Jesus to watch someone he loved make such a catastrophically wrong choice. But Jesus *respected* the young man's God-given gift of free will.

Our Lord, who would soon give up his life to rescue humankind and who could command the very wind and waves to obey his voice, chose not to compel this man—not even for his own good. We should follow his example. Without a foundation of this kind of Christlike respect, even genuine caring and authentic understanding can quickly become condescending, self-righteous, and parental. Without respect, we're all too ready to control and manipulate even those we genuinely love and understand. And in today's postmodern culture, there is probably no sin that is more offensive and repelling to the people we want to reach. Why are Christians characterized as being rude, arrogant, and pushy? Because we haven't offered non-Christians this kind of Christlike respect.

This is why Philippians 2:3 says, "Do nothing out of selfish ambition or vain conceit, but in humility consider others *better than yourselves*" (emphasis added). We are called to respect everyone Christ gave his life to save—even more than we respect ourselves. Respect means we don't assume we can or should provide all the answers. We don't patronize or condescend as we listen. Instead, we help people understand and take responsibility for their own problems. Followers of Jesus have to realize that this kind of respect can never be earned; rather, it must be freely given to all. Trust, on the other hand, *must be earned.* Those to whom we listen reward us with their trust as we consistently demonstrate Christlike respect.

Burdens and Loads

Wait just one minute. Doesn't Galatians 6:2 say we're supposed to bear one another's burdens? Doesn't that mean we are supposed to take responsibility for weaker brothers and sisters? The answer is no. We are called to be considerate and to offer help when others' problems are more overwhelming than they can handle alone but never to take away their God-given responsibility. Doing so is the deepest and most profound insult we can possibly commit against someone who is not physically or mentally incapacitated. We discuss this issue at significant length in our book *Listening for Heaven's Sake* and its companion course.[9] To summarize two lengthy chapters from that book very briefly: We are all responsible *to* others, but ultimately they are responsible *for* themselves.

This is a hard truth for many leaders, especially for those with the Parent and Performer temperaments we will discuss in Chapters 9 and 10. When Galatians 6:2 says to bear one another's burdens, we tend to interpret it to mean that we should do their work *for* them. Dr. Henry Cloud and Dr. John Townsend dispel this misconception in their book *Boundaries.* According to Cloud and Townsend, "We are responsible *to* others and *for* ourselves. 'Carry each other's burdens,' says Galatians 6:2, 'and in this way you will fulfill the law of Christ.' This verse shows our responsibility *to* one another."[10]

The New Testament word translated as "burdens" is *baros.* It means a weight too heavy or a difficulty too severe to be handled by one person by himself or herself. Cloud and Townsend speak of burdens being like boulders in a farmer's field that are too massive for him to move by himself. The "boulders" of life are those obstacles we can only overcome with help. For example, it's common practice in many families for a parent to move in for a few days in order to help a new mother who's just had a baby. The parent takes care of running the household while the new mom concentrates on recovering from the stresses of childbirth. At first, sharing the extra burdens of motherhood with grandma can be a great relief, but before too many days pass, the new mother is usually ready to send the helper home and begin running her own household again.

When grandmas and new moms allow healthy burden-bearing to turn into unhealthy dependency, the result is resentment that can go both ways. The one who is over-functioning increasingly resents the one who is under-functioning for being lazy or weak. Even though the under-functioning mom may revel in the attention and concern lavished on her at first, she will also quickly grow to resent the overly helpful ministrations that put her back into a childlike role. A discerning grandma will read the signs that it's time to go.

Galatians 6 says something that, on the surface, seems a bit contradictory. Speaking directly to the dependency issues we've just been talking about, Galatians 6:5 reads, "Each one should carry *his own* load" (emphasis added). So which is it? Should leaders be compassionate burden-bearers or uncompromising practitioners of tough love?

Of course, the answer is "yes!" There are times when people need compassionate help with things that are too hard for them to carry, and then there is the rest of the time when they must shoulder their responsibilities on their own. Cloud and Townsend compare the load of responsibility that rightfully belongs to every person to a knapsack. It's a personal gift from God that is theirs and theirs alone. Taking it away from them even for the most seemingly kindhearted reasons is the most degrading form of theft imaginable. If grandma insists on doing all the diaper-changing, bathing, and baby-holding, she has taken over her daughter's role as a mother...even if the mother is a teenager or already has four children to care for.

So how does Christlike respect translate in practical terms for the quick-to-listen leader? Christlike respect assumes that people are responsible for their own choices and for facing the consequences that come with them. It recognizes the awesome gift and the terrible responsibility of another's free will. In the following chapter, we'll discover ways to use the proactive listening skills of question-asking and focused self-disclosure to demonstrate Christlike respect.

ENDNOTES

1. Although Carl Rogers pioneered active listening as part of his client-centered therapy approach, many others have built on the foundation he laid. We are deeply indebted to Robert Carkhuff and Gerard Egan for systematizing the practice for use in counseling, medical, and caring professions. For more information, see Carl R. Rogers and David Russell, *Carl Rogers: The Quiet Revolutionary, An Oral History* (Roseville, CA: Penmarin Books, 2002); Robert R. Carkhuff, *The Art of Helping in the 21st Century* (Amherst, MA: Human Resource Development Press, Inc., 2000); Gerard Egan, *The Skilled Helper: A Systematic Approach to Effective Helping* (Monterey, CA: Brooks/Cole Publishing Company, 1986).

2. Paul Tournier, *A Place for You: Psychology and Religion* (New York, NY: Harper & Row, 1968). Paul Tournier, *A Listening Ear: Reflections on Christian Caring* (Minneapolis, MN: Augsburg Publishing House, 1987).

3. Gary R. Collins, *The Christian Psychology of Paul Tournier* (Grand Rapids, MI: Baker Book House, 1973). Gary R. Collins, *Christian Counseling: A Comprehensive Guide, Revised Edition* (Waco, TX: Word Publishing, 1988). Gary R. Collins, *Can You Trust Psychology?: Exposing the Facts & the Fictions* (Downers Grove, IL: InterVarsity Press, 1988). Gary R. Collins, *Christian Coaching: Helping Others Turn Potential Into Reality* (Colorado Springs, CO: NavPress, 2001).

4. Larry Crabb, *Connecting: Healing for Ourselves and Our Relationships: A Radical New Vision* (Nashville, TN: Word Publishing, 1997). Larry Crabb, *The Safest Place on Earth: Where People Connect and Are Forever Changed* (Nashville, TN: Word Publishing, 1999).

5. Paul D. Meier, Frank B. Minirth, Frank B. Wichern, and Donald E. Ratcliff, *Introduction to Psychology and Counseling: Christian Perspectives and Applications* (Grand Rapids, MI: Baker Book House, 1991). Paul Meier, *Don't Let Jerks Get the Best of You* (Nashville, TN: Thomas Nelson, Inc., 1993). Frank Minirth and Paul Meier, *Happiness Is a Choice: The Symptoms, Causes, and Cures of Depression* (Grand Rapids, MI: Baker Books, 1994). Stephen Arterburn, Frank B. Minirth, and Paul Meier, *Safe Places: Finding Security in the Passages of Your Life* (Nashville, TN: Thomas Nelson Publishers, 1997).

6. George M. Gazda, William C. Childers, and Richard P. Walters, *Interpersonal Communication: A Handbook for Health Professionals* (Rockville, MD: Aspen Systems Corporation, 1982). Richard P. Walters, *How to Be a Friend People Want to Be Friends With* (Ventura, CA: Regal Books, 1981). Richard P. Walters *Forgive and Be Free: Healing the Wounds of Past and Present* (Grand Rapids, MI: Zondervan Publishing House, 1983). Richard P. Walters, *Counseling for Problems of Self-Control* (Waco, TX: Word Books, 1987).

7. Gary Sweeten, Dave Ping, and Anne Clippard, *Listening for Heaven's Sake: Building Healthy Relationships With God, Self and Others* (Cincinnati, OH: Teleios Publications, 1993).

8. Albert Mehrabian, *Silent Messages: Implicit Communication of Emotions and Attitudes* (Belmont, CA: Wadsworth Publishing Company, 1981).

9. Equipping Ministries International has developed a ten-hour interactive training to help church staff and lay people learn and practice the essentials of Christ-like active listening.

10. Henry Cloud and John Townsend, *Boundaries: When to Say Yes, When to Say No to Take Control of Your Life* (Grand Rapids, MI: Zondervan Publishing House, 1992), 30.

▮▮▮ Feeling-Words Finder ▮▮▮

Mad

MORE → LESS

Outraged, Infuriated, Furious, Unforgiving, Bitter, Exasperated, Enraged, Revengeful, Resentful, Incensed, Aggrieved, Indignant, Appalled, Revolted, Nauseated, Revulsed, Repulsed, Disgusted, Fed up, Livid, Burned up, Heated, Angry, Frustrated, Disturbed, Offended, Peeved, Put out, Perturbed, Ticked off, Piqued, Displeased, Irked, Annoyed, Provoked, Aggravated, Agitated, Irritated, Uptight, Upset, Miffed, Bothered

Sad

MORE → LESS

Distraught, Devastated, Inconsolable, Desolate, Hopeless, Despairing, Depressing, Wretched, Crushed, Dejected, Defeated, Despondent, Dreadful, Miserable, Terrible, Lousy, Grieved, Disgruntled, Dissatisfied, Discontented, Empty, Forlorn, Gloomy, Dismayed, Distressed, Downhearted, Melancholy, Washed-out, Tired, Exhausted, Worn out, Saddened, Thwarted, Disillusioned, Disenchanted, Let-down, Disappointed, Lost, Low, Unhappy, Somber, Blue, Down

Glad

MORE → LESS

Ecstatic, Overjoyed, Wonderful, Elated, Exhilarated, Thrilled, Excited, Terrific, Tickled, Delighted, Moved, Inspired, Motivated, Stimulated, Proud, Upbeat, Hopeful, Positive, Optimistic, Expectant, Confident, Encouraged, Recharged, Rejuvenated, Revived, Energized, Revitalized, Invigorated, Refreshed, Joyful, Cheerful, Happy, Pleased, Satisfied, Gratified, Contented, Peaceful, Tranquil, Relaxed, Comfortable, Secure, Composed, Calm, At ease

Afraid

MORE → LESS

Hysterical, Terrified, Petrified, Horrified, Stricken, Out of control, Panicky, Frantic, Freaked-out, Overwhelmed, Numb, Stunned, Shocked, Agitated, Startled, Shaken, Frightened, Fearful, Scared, Troubled, Concerned, Worried, Unnerved, Distraught, Distressed, Alarmed, On edge, Uptight, Disturbed, Stressed, Nervous, Anxious, Wound-up, Stirred-up, Tense, Hesitant, Abashed, Chagrined, Uncomfortable, Cautious, Bothered, Insecure, Embarrassed, Apprehensive, Ill-at-ease, Uneasy

Ashamed

MORE → LESS

Wretched, Degraded, Devastated, Defiled, Scandalized, Mortified, Unclean, Despoiled, Depolled, Tarnished, Tainted, Corrupted, Polluted, Dirty, Violated, Sickened, Revolted, Disgusted, Desecrated, Dishonored, Debased, Accountable, Blameworthy, Offended, Responsible, Guilty, Abstracted, Unfocused, Distracted, Affronted, Remorseful, Regretful, Apologetic, Sorry, Confounded, Mystified, Disgraced, Humiliated, Branded, Dismayed, Unsettled, Ambivalent, Indecisive, Tentative, Hesitant, Doubtful, Unsure, Undecided, Uncertain

Confused

MORE → LESS

Flabbergasted, Shocked, Dumbfounded, Stunned, Worn out, Torn, Lost, Muddled, Surprised, Astonished, Dazed, Dismayed, Split, Disjointed, Fragmented, Disconcerted, Flustered, Sidetracked, Diverted, Detached, Insignificant, Out of place, Preoccupied, Unforced, Distracted, Befuddled, Bewildered, Bemused, Baffled, Confounded, Puzzled, Perplexed, Unresolved, Unsettled, Ambivalent, Indecisive, Tentative, Hesitant, Doubtful, Unsure, Undecided, Uncertain

"Then we will no longer be infants, tossed back and forth by the waves, and blown here and there by every wind of teaching and by the cunning and craftiness of men in their deceitful scheming. Instead, speaking the truth in love, we will in all things grow up into him who is the Head, that is, Christ. From him the whole body, joined and held together by every supporting ligament, grows and builds itself up in love, as each part does its work" (Ephesians 4:14-16).

6

Get Out There
AND LISTEN!

As helpful as Christlike active listening is, there's a lot more to learn as we seek to become quick to listen and slow to speak. As we alluded to earlier, *active* listening is just the beginning. If we want to lead as effectively as possible, we have to learn to be *proactive*. After all, healthy leaders are able to take initiative instead of merely reacting as Ephesians 4:14 describes, like "infants, tossed back and forth by the waves, and blown here and there by every wind of teaching and by the cunning and craftiness of men in their deceitful scheming."

If you've ever tried to follow a reactive leader, you know how frustrating and exhausting it can be for everyone involved. With fingers forever wetted and thrust up in the air to test every subtle shift in wind direction, we end up chasing all the latest trends and fancies. When the attraction of one movement begins to wane, another comes along to propel us elsewhere. For a while, this blowing and drifting process can be fun and even stimulating. We get to visit interesting places and learn fascinating things. We get to talk to the latest consultants and hear inspiring gurus. In the process we spend all our precious time and money drifting in every direction and ultimately going nowhere.

For a club or a movie theater whose purpose is solely entertainment, there is nothing wrong with this approach. But for a church whose purpose is to "go and make disciples of all nations, baptizing them in the name of the Father and of the Son and of the Holy Spirit, and teaching them to obey everything I [Jesus] have commanded you" (Matthew 28:19-20a), this fluid, amorphous approach is certainly not the way to go. If our primary purpose is to make disciples (rather than simply providing fulfilling leisure activities to bored churchgoers), discipleship is the fundamental objective that needs to drive everything—even, and perhaps especially, our listening.

These days it's common to hear of purpose-driven churches and purpose-driven lives, but what about *purpose-driven listening*? Isn't it time to talk about how proactive listening, building trust, sharing ourselves, and "speaking the truth in love" allow us to equip more fully devoted disciples of Jesus? Of course it is! That's why you are reading this book. Building on the attitudes and skills we've discussed in previous chapters, we are now going to suggest ways you can use listening to *seek out* and intentionally engage others in the essential processes of Christian discipleship.

Proactive Seeking

Leadership has little to do with studious isolation and everything to do with how we connect with ordinary people.

Deep-rooted myths about Christian leaders envisage hermitlike sages poring over obscure texts and occasionally meeting with other big-brained spiritual giants in private studies up high in their ivy-covered ivory towers. (Say that three times fast: "Ivy-covered ivory towers, ivy-covered ivory towers, ivy-covered ivory towers!") Safe in our hideaways, we think deep thoughts and write down powerful words designed to stir the masses below into action. Once a week (or twice, if we're from more conservative churches), we descend the stairs and passionately deliver meticulously crafted words to expectant crowds who will be awed and transformed by the very hearing of them.

It's time to dispel that myth, get real, and come down to earth! Leadership has little to do with studious isolation and everything to do with how we connect with ordinary people. "The meat is in the street," as the Jesus People used to say, but most of us don't operate with this understanding. Too many leaders are trapped in offices and glued to telephones and computers. We attend endless rounds of wearisome meetings and an occasional conference or two, but otherwise we hardly ever get out.

As leaders, we rarely take time to hang out with the modern-day fishermen, shepherds, and tax collectors who could someday become disciples who turn the world upside down. If we stay trapped in the old mythology of the isolated leader, we won't put ourselves in situations in which we can actively listen to and build trust with the ordinary car dealers, accountants, and postal workers who populate our communities and congregations. We're not talking about the folks who come to us for counseling or serve with us on various committees. Certainly we ought to listen to these people, but since they come to us, listening to them doesn't require us to be proactive in the same way.

Proactive listening means intentionally going where people are and seeking to understand what's happening in their worlds without waiting for an engraved invitation. It's almost as simple as learning how to say, "Hey, I'd like to get together and hear what's going on with you." We say "almost" because the words mean nothing if your attitude and motivation are wrong.

Proactive listening is not the same as being nice or seeming interested in people so we can get what we want from them. It's intentional and genuine. These two things go together only when the intentions are unselfish. If you listen only to increase your church membership, to raise money, to gather influence, or to recruit people to teach Sunday school, people will see right through you. They will see you as one more peddler in the long line of other salespeople who want to win their business.

> If you listen only to increase your church membership, to raise money, to gather influence, or to recruit people to teach Sunday school, people will see right through you. They will see you as one more peddler in the long line of other salespeople who want to win their business.

The trick to proactive listening, if there is one, is that genuine love comes first. (Come, Holy Spirit!) When we seek to love God with all we have and care about our neighbors as we do ourselves (Matthew 22:37-39), all these things that build up God's people and his church will be given to us (Matthew 6:33). In other words, when we genuinely love people and listen to them, God takes care of the rest.

Not everyone to whom we extend our friendship and our ears will become a disciple, but when we sow the caring seeds of God's kingdom in genuine, nonmanipulative ways, they're never wasted. In fact, they have an amazing tendency to pop up in the most unexpected times and places. Some leaders have been taught that being strategic means focusing all our attention on "influencers" and not wasting precious time on people who don't produce the results we're seeking. This may be good business, but in our experience, God delights in lifting up and using the least likely people most powerfully.

Our worldwide ministry began with thirty people in the basement of College Hill Presbyterian Church. All of them were struggling and broken in different ways. Some were recovering from painful divorces or family breakdowns, others were wounded or unemployed, and still others were suffering from clinical depression or trying to overcome homosexual temptations and leave the "gay" lifestyle. As the seeds of genuine caring fell into their lives, the growth and the fruit they produced were nothing short of miraculous. Not only did these few broken people experience tremendous healing and growth, but some of the most broken among them became powerful disciples and trainers who have led thousands to healing. These unlikely leadership candidates and the people they've discipled have now trained over 100,000 people to serve the Lord more effectively.

What would happen if "let's do lunch" was a way to actively pursue conversation? Try setting up times to meet people at a restaurant, in their homes, or anywhere they feel comfortable talking. *Get out there!* Then be quick to listen and slow to speak. Keep the conversational spotlight on the other person's agenda without pushing for your own. If you listen proactively, respectfully, and warmly, you'll be surprised how much people appreciate it and will open up to you about their hopes and fears and dreams.

Here's an example. Dale, a director in a parachurch ministry, had been spending his spare time checking on the construction workers who were helping build his family's new home. Since he usually visited around lunchtime, he asked if next time he could bring lunch and take some time to get to know the guys on a personal level. They not only agreed but loved doing it. Because Dale listened, these tough, mostly non-Christian men opened up and talked about all sorts of things, from family issues to their beliefs about God. Dale was intrigued and asked if he could bring his pastor to lunch so they could tell him what they thought about church. The men said, "Sure, as long as he doesn't mind hearing what we really think."

Lunch with the construction crew was an eye-opening experience for Dale's pastor. He had to bite his tongue several times to keep from preaching at or arguing with the workers as they talked about how they perceived Christians and the church. Eventually, as he patiently listened, the workers realized he was there as a listener and a learner. By the time lunch was over, everyone was having so much fun talking that they asked if the pastor could come back again. They'd never met a preacher who was so friendly and who didn't condemn them or preach the truth at them.

For his part, the pastor got a whole new understanding of how some ordinary, nonreligious Joes perceived God. He realized that getting out of his office and really listening was one of the smartest things he could do to grow his church. Interestingly enough, when one of the guys from the crew faced a crisis in his family, the first place he turned was to Dale and his pastor.

When you begin to listen proactively, people around you will usually begin to

▌ enjoy talking to you more.

▌ feel more accepted by you.

▌ become less suspicious of your motivations.

▌ start to trust your concern for them.

▌ open up and tell you more about what's important to them.

▌ seek you out when they need advice.

▌ use you as a sounding board about feelings and big decisions.

▌ want to understand why you care and listen the way you do.

▌ become interested in connecting with you and the things you care about.

These relational developments signal a budding camaraderie that is headed in the direction of real friendship and, with the Holy Spirit's help, perhaps real discipleship. Even if you started reading this book as a relational "grinch," judging those who think and feel differently, with God's help you will find your concern for people expanding day by day if you proactively seek to listen. As John Ortberg says, "The more spiritually mature you grow, the more you will find your heart being drawn to people...especially those neglected by society or far from God."[1] In other words, as you grow closer to Christ, you will become more and more intentional about connecting with the people *he* cares about. This is discipleship too. As we follow our Master, we will grow more and more like him.

Five Kinds of Questions

When we talk about proactive listening, we mean *intentionally seeking* opportunities to initiate and pursue conversations in which we will listen more than we talk. Instead of waiting around for people to come to us and open their hearts, we deliberately work to create opportunities for listening relationships to happen. It's evangelistic in the most positive sense of the word because we reach out to where others are and build bridges into their worlds. One of the basic tools for making the first contacts that lead into listening conversations is the ability to ask good questions.

1. Connecting Questions

Most of the common questions we ask are designed to do one of five things. The first familiar function that questions serve is to initiate a conversation. We all know lots of standard opening questions such as "How are you today?" or "Is it hot enough for you?" Asking these types of questions is like throwing another person a rope we hope he or she will pick up and use to connect with us.

Most good conversation-starting questions are innocuous and nonthreatening. They are not overly familiar, nor do they suggest that we are seeking anything other than a friendly chat. Initiating conversation is something many extroverts do naturally. Elizabeth, the most extroverted friend we have, doesn't hesitate to walk up to perfect strangers and say, "Hello, my name is Beth. What's yours?" or "I was noticing that you were reading a book about listening for leaders; what made you pick that up?" Since it's clear Beth is genuinely interested, most people receive her conversational bids warmly and gladly strike up a conversation with her. She's so good at it that she puts people at ease without even thinking.

If you're not as outgoing as Beth, you probably *do* have to think about the opening questions you want to ask and work up the courage to ask them. Proactively inviting connection doesn't come naturally for everyone, but it is something anyone who wants to care about others can learn. That's Beth's secret. She genuinely cares about the people around her and wants to connect with them. Her manner and expression communicate interest and warmth, and then her words open the door to a positive conversation. The words don't matter as much as the attitude with which they're spoken. In John 4:7, Jesus began one of the most powerful conversations in the New Testament by simply asking a woman at a well, "Will you give me a drink?"

> The words don't matter as much as the attitude with which they're spoken.

For those of us on the shy end of the spectrum, it may be more challenging to tune in to the caring the Lord feels for the people we meet. As we go about the day-to-day business of picking up groceries, going to the gym, watching our children's activities, or getting our hair cut, we can practice the "ministry of noticing" and initiating conversations with the people around us. You will be surprised how positively most people respond when you break the silence to make a connection. Simply step out in faith and say, "Hello, my name is [Martin or Sue or whatever]. How are you today?" They will probably say, "I'm [Alvin or Eliza], and I'm fine, thank you" or something equally bland. Once they've determined that you're not selling anything, conversations naturally progress to open-ended questions that show we are interested. "How'd you get started cutting hair?" or "You're obviously into diet and fitness. What would you tell someone who's just getting started?" or "What caused you to move to this town?"

▌▌▌ Rent an Extrovert

If you're not sure how to do and say the kinds of things we've been talking about, try "renting" an extrovert. Invite a naturally outgoing friend to lunch, and ask him or her to tell you how he or she connects with people and initiates conversations. This person will most likely feel honored to be treated as your personal connecting expert. Follow your friend around and observe a few conversations.

You probably won't be able to do it as naturally at first, but try one or two of the things you see working anyway. It may feel funny at first, but because connecting with others is a skill, you can learn it and get better at it.

Connecting questions have many variations but only one theme: to encourage people to talk about what's important to them. Once they start talking, we can use the Christlike active listening skills described in the last chapter to support and encourage them on their journey. The luxury of sharing this kind of exploration tends to bring insight, release, and refreshment to people. Most people love having a genuinely friendly person to talk to and don't view it as an intrusion.

> Have you known teachers or supervisors who have proactively expressed genuine interest in you with no agenda other than caring? If you have, you know just how powerful these simple gestures can be.

This open-ended approach also works well for leaders who want to develop deeper connections with the people around them. You can invite people you lead (or are interested in relating with) to lunch or take a fifteen-minute break to focus on getting to know them better. As long as it's clear that you don't have ulterior motives, most people will enjoy sharing their thoughts with you and start to see you as someone who's *on their team.* Have you known teachers or supervisors who have proactively expressed genuine interest in you with no agenda other than caring? If you have, you know just how powerful these simple gestures can be. These genuinely interested leaders are often the people who have changed the course of our lives and inspired us in new directions.

2. Condescending Questions

A second and less positive function of asking questions is to assert control and establish authority in a conversation. Anyone who has been a student has been conditioned to respond deferentially to these kinds of questions. The questioner is usually a parent, teacher, principal, or some other authority figure, and we are expected to provide him or her with the "right" answer. When a teacher asks, "What is five times five?" we know we're supposed to raise our hands and say, "Twenty-five!" When a Christian leader asks, "Who do you think created the universe?" most folks know that they are expected to answer, "God!" Our students may or may not choose to answer according to our expectations, but they feel them (and often resent them) all the same.

For parents and Christian leaders alike, this type of question can be deadly. When people see us as authority figures who must be pleased and placated, they usually tell us exactly what they think *we want to hear*. The teen who hears his parent say, "Is there going to be alcohol at this party?" knows that if he wants to attend, the answer must be "Of course not!" In this case, parents are asserting their authority more than asking a question. This can also happen in churches. We've been to churches where the proper response to the question "How are you?" is "I'm highly blessed and favored, Brother So-and-So!" Any derivation from this expected answer is likely to result in a good-natured lecture. As we move toward Christlike listening, we need to make it clear that we are more interested in real feelings and thoughts than we are in hearing any "right" answer. If we want to see real results, we have to start where people really are and not where we want them to be.

> If we want to see real results, we have to start where people really are and not where we want them to be.

3. Controlling Questions

Controlling questions steer the conversation where we want it to go instead of where the person speaking is currently taking it. We may be curious about details or anxious about where the conversation is headed. So we try to redirect it to satisfy our own needs. No problem, right? No. Big problem! Imagine how you'd feel if you were driving down the highway and the person in the passenger's seat suddenly grabbed the steering wheel and forced the car to exit. Yikes! This situation would not only be scary but also would tend to put more than a little stress into the passenger-driver relationship.

In real life, someone who can't control the urge to hijack the steering wheel doesn't often get a second ride. Unfortunately, the scenario we've just described is very common in the world of listening. Have you ever tried to pour out your heart to someone only to have the conversation wrenched away from your planned course by an over-inquisitive or self-absorbed conversational hijacker? These controlling listeners may be well-intentioned and even loving people most of the time, but when they give in to the urge to take over, we feel disrespected and are reluctant to continue trusting them.

As the listener, think of yourself as the passenger rather than the driver of the conversation. Your job is to buckle up and ride wherever the driver takes you. However, there *are* times a conversational passenger may need to make his or her boundaries known. Before you hit the road and begin a conversation, it might be respectful to say, "I have forty-five minutes I can give you right now; will that work for you?" If you find yourself in the middle of a conversation and realize that the driver won't make it to the destination in the time you have available, say, "It seems pretty clear that you have a lot more to say, and I have only fifteen minutes before my next meeting. Will that be enough time for you to finish your thought?" If the driver says "no," you can spend the remaining time arranging another time to finish the conversation. The key to proactive listening is being honest and respectful rather than controlling.

Proactive listeners pay attention to where the speaker is headed. They allow the speaker to control the gas pedal that determines the pace of the conversation and the steering wheel that rules its direction. In proactive listening, the listener clarifies what the speaker is saying without attempting to steer the conversation in a whole new direction. This is a hard discipline for everyone but especially for most leaders. However, it's a discipline worth mastering. When you try it, you'll discover that listeners who are allowed to steer feel more trusted and responsible—and often travel willingly to places we could never steer them.

A lady named Sarah came into the counseling ministry where I (Anne) volunteer. Sarah wanted to try to understand some issues that seemed to be keeping her from experiencing abundant life in her ministry. She appeared to be very unassuming and humble. But as Sarah talked and I listened, Sarah began to identify a root of pride that had held her captive many times during her lifetime. This insight would never have been identified if I had taken the lead and directed the conversation the way I wanted it to go. The more Sarah talked about different situations in her life, the more she realized that her pride had kept her from trying new things. Because of her pride, Sarah was afraid of failure and worried what other people might think of her. After she had identified and surrendered this problem to God, God gave her a new excitement about stepping out in faith to accomplish his will.

4. Clarifying Questions

Clarifying questions open up new possibilities as a speaker considers his or her own thoughts and feelings. On the road of listening, clarifying questions are like a friend getting out a map and saying, "Is this the route you want to take, or are you interested in this one?" As long as we ask at the right time and don't lobby too hard for a particular route, people will thank us for asking. Clarifying questions are useful when people begin to repeat themselves and seem to have lost their focus or when they begin to have insights that lead them to natural crossroads or turning points.

Clarifying is at the heart of listening. It's checking in to make sure you're tracking with what's being said and you understand where people want to go. As you clarify, be careful that your questions don't lead you to be controlling or argumentative. There is a time for confronting and disagreeing, but usually it's best and, in our experience, much faster to listen thoroughly first. Clarifying questions help people understand themselves better. And, as an added benefit, when people are clear in their own minds, they are much more receptive to listening to other points of view.

5. Wondering Questions

The fifth function of asking questions is uncommon. It's one many leaders discover only after years of working to motivate individuals and teams to think for themselves. We call it *active wondering.*[2] It means listening well enough to pose questions that cause the other person to begin actively wondering about new possibilities.

There are all sorts of wondering questions, and most begin with the simple words "As we've been talking, I've been wondering…" You can wonder about what a person is thinking or feeling. You can wonder how the person has come to believe what he or she believes or to do what he or she does. We might say something like "As we've been talking, I've been wondering…

▪ how did you choose your current career?"

▪ what's been the biggest influence in your life up till now?"

▪ how would you describe your unique purpose in life?"

▪ what do you think heaven might be like, if there is one?"

Wondering flows from the context of your conversation, so good listening is essential. The possibilities are endless, and, of course, some wondering questions are far more helpful than others. As people respond to these questions, avoid judging or condemning their answers. If, later on, you feel you need to confront an error in the speaker's thinking, you will be far more effective if you thoroughly understand what the person really believes and why. Wondering questions can help you truly understand the speaker. How often should you ask them? It's almost always wise to err on the side of listening and wondering too much rather than too little.

A good wondering question has four essential components. *First, it is nonthreatening.* Most people are on guard against anything that smells like a sales pitch. They fear being caught up and swept along in someone else's personal agenda. We've all met bosses who've operated by the slogan "God loves you, and I have a wonderful plan for your life." They have grand strategies about how they can use our gifts, talents, and time to make themselves look good. If you've ever been used in this way, you're probably careful of any question that sounds like it might lead to a prefabricated conclusion that will benefit the asker more than it will benefit you.

> No matter how true they might be, predigested absolutes are as dead as dirt, and conclusions we reach and discover personally are alive.

Second, effective wondering questions communicate humility. Asking questions for which you have no set answers is anti-arrogant in its very nature. It elevates the person with whom you are talking to expert status about what he or she believes and feels.

Third, wondering questions allow others to discover their own answers. Before you freak out and decide that we've embraced moral relativism, we should probably point out that not all answers are true or equal. But the answer I find for myself is more personal and powerful than anything someone else could tell me. No matter how true they might be, predigested absolutes are as dead as dirt, and conclusions we reach and discover personally are alive. One of the reasons Jesus taught in parables was so his hearers could draw living conclusions for themselves.

Great wondering questions challenge people to engage in their own search for truth. Jesus himself promised, "Ask and it will be given to you; seek and you will find; knock and the door will be opened to you. For everyone who asks receives; he who seeks finds; and to him who knocks, the door will be opened" (Matthew 7:7-8; Luke 11:9-10). Once we help people become seekers, they will be well on their way to finding what God wants to show them.

Last, great wondering questions lead to new ways of thinking and more exciting questions. Wonder leads to wonder, and seeking leads to finding, and the whole process of listening leads us deeper and closer to God. Hallelujah! Isn't that the goal of both evangelism and discipleship—to draw people into a deeper life-giving relationship with God?

Being quick to listen means initiating and connecting with people—all kinds of people, all the time. Surprisingly, introverts actually have a natural advantage in this area. Because whether or not you can get them to admit it, introverts are constantly wondering about the people around them. Though they may not always appear interested, they often harbor a burning curiosity about what makes others tick. Unlike their extroverted friends, introverts tend to pay close attention to the words and subtle nonverbal cues others are communicating. Secretly they wonder, "What must it be like to be that person?" or "How does that person cope with the stress he or she is under?" They ask themselves hundreds of other good questions that never pass their lips.

▌▌▌ Rent an Introvert

If you're having trouble thinking of good wondering questions, it might help to "rent" an introvert. Invite an introverted friend to lunch, and talk about the people questions that go through his or her head. You will be surprised at the detailed internal thought processes many introverts use to observe people. Introverts also naturally tune in to signs that tell them when they might be intruding on someone's space. While introverts may be over-sensitive to these things, many extroverts miss them all together. This capacity for other-centered wondering is a powerful gift introverts rarely get to unwrap and use to its full potential.

Both introverts and extroverts can become better at initiating and enhancing listening conversations without dominating them. To practice the skill of active wondering, both of them need to stretch. We have so much to learn from each other!

Finding the Brakes and the Gas Pedal

Although extroverts can start conversations with complete strangers without batting an eye, they often talk more than they listen and tend to focus more on their own thoughts and feelings. When I (Dave) have conversations with friends over dinner, my introverted wife, Pam, is constantly stepping on my feet under the table.

When Pam steps on my feet, it's her way of "tapping the brake" and prompting me to quit talking so much and start focusing more on our friends. Since we've been married, the tops of my shoes have worn out nearly as fast as the soles. But all humor aside, I've learned to appreciate and even anticipate Pam's prompting as she effortlessly tunes in to nonverbal signals that I have to concentrate on in order to see.

On the flip side, Pam is often too shy to speak up about the insightful wondering questions that come into her mind. After dinner she might say, "As we were talking to Bill and Anne, I was wondering such and such." I just shake my head, bemoaning the exciting but missed opportunity her unasked question represents.

Lately, I've taken to gently stepping on her *foot during conversations with friends. One of the best ways I've found to do this is to stop my own train of thought and ask her, "Did you have a thought you would like to share?" In her case, it's not the brake but the gas pedal I'm hitting.*

Self-Disclosure

In addition to proactive seeking and asking good questions, *focused self-disclosure* can help us move higher up and deeper in to the lives of the people around us. In focused self-disclosure, we encourage people to open up by giving them a glimpse of our own lives—failings, struggles, and shortcomings included. Sounds like barrels of fun, right? Let's disclose the things we are least proud of to someone who, up till now, thinks we are pretty smart and at least marginally together. Why on earth would we want to do that?

> Self-disclosure is one of the best ways of transmitting God's comfort into the lives of others.

Honest self-disclosure allows us to share the real insights and wisdom we've gained from our struggles. Done appropriately, it gives others hope, helps them face their own struggles with less shame, and gives them insight into possible new directions when they're stuck.

In 2 Corinthians 1:3-4, Paul speaks of "the Father of compassion and the God of all comfort, who comforts us in all our troubles, so that we can comfort those in any trouble with the comfort we ourselves have received from God." Self-disclosure is one of the best ways of transmitting God's comfort into the lives of others. The New Testament word for *comfort* in this verse has multiple meanings beyond merely helping someone feel better. *Comfort* also means to encourage, to exhort, and to invite. It means coming alongside another person as an equal and a fellow struggler.

Focused self-disclosure can elevate your listening skills to a much higher, more personal level. Unfortunately, it can also subject you to unfair criticism and gossip. This is a valid concern. More than a few leaders have confided a personal failing to someone they trusted, only to have it used against them later. This sort of betrayal is the reason many leaders have been taught *never* to confess personal thoughts, fears, or struggles to their followers.

But in spite of this very real risk, we still think self-disclosure, when used appropriately, is important. Why? Because it helps dispel the widely held but false conviction that leaders should be "practically perfect in every way," as the fantasy character Mary Poppins said. Of course, we all aspire to be the best leaders we can be. But the idea that people will follow us only if they perceive us to be paragons of every virtue is a dangerous one indeed. It puts leaders on a pedestal beyond the reach of normal mortals (which, of course, we all are). This approach is not only unhealthy but also unbiblical and unsustainable. Every pedestal and every false image will eventually be toppled, and it's usually best for us to do the toppling ourselves. As we swear off pretending, we become not only more approachable but also more powerful leaders.

As we've already said, focused self-disclosure, when used appropriately, will help you take your relationships to a higher, deeper level. Sadly, self-disclosure is also one of the most frequently misused

> Every pedestal and every false image will eventually be toppled, and it's usually best for us to do the toppling ourselves. As we swear off pretending, we become not only more approachable but also more powerful leaders.

and abused communication tools we know. We've all suffered through lengthy expositions that begin with "That reminds me of a time..." or "When I was your age..." So how do we use self-disclosure appropriately to draw people closer rather than send them screaming from the room?

Self-Disclosure Secrets

There are four simple secrets that will keep your self-disclosures helpful, brief, and on target.

Secret 1: When the Time Is Right

First, self-disclosure is only helpful when it is done at the right time in the conversation. If you sense that a person is beating around the bush in an attempt to acknowledge an embarrassing feeling, you might briefly self-disclose by saying, "If I were in your place, I would probably feel _____. I wonder if that's how you're feeling now." The speaker will either agree with you and expand on what you've said or clarify and correct it. Either way, your self-disclosure will facilitate his or her emotional exploration and provide new insight.

Self-disclosure also helps when people feel alone or hopeless in their struggles. One pastor we know decided to disclose in a sermon that he had been sexually abused as a child. Several colleagues warned him against it, but he did it anyway.

In the sermon he shared how counseling was helping him overcome feelings of shame he had felt all his life. At the end of his message, he announced that the church was starting a support group for people who'd had similar experiences. He expected thirty or forty people at the first session, but hundreds came. The most common comment he heard at the meeting and received via e-mail was "I thought I was the only one." By his courageous example, he showed how being vulnerable while staying positive and honest can lead to amazing hope and freedom.

Another key time to self-disclose is when people feel stuck or can't see any alternatives to a potentially hurtful or destructive pattern in their lives. In these times, your self-disclosure can help people examine other possibilities. When a friend told Anne she was on the verge of leaving her husband, Anne told her about some times she'd made the mistake of hastily saying and doing things that couldn't be unsaid or undone. She told her friend, "I've learned to bite my tongue in the moment and take plenty of time to thoroughly count the costs my words might have on me and my family. I wonder if taking some time to examine the costs of leaving your marriage could help you make the kind of decision you won't regret later."

Secret 2: Keep It Brief, Keep It Relevant

Once you're fairly sure it's a good time for self-disclosure, *briefly relate a relevant personal experience, feeling, or insight you've had.* Recognize that your experience will never be exactly the same as your partner's, but gently point out any similarities you think will be helpful. You don't have to be divorced or an alcoholic or have had an extramarital affair to have experiences or feelings that might help clarify your partner's feelings in these situations. You do need to be sensitive and listen even more carefully after you self-disclose.

Secret 3: Equality Is the Best Policy

Third, remember to relate as an equal. People feel much more respected when we don't come across like a parent or an expert. You are not a judge dispensing a verdict or an older brother looking down in a way that says, "I told you so." Even if the other person is facing a huge, scary problem you'd never expect to encounter yourself, remember: "There, but by the grace of God, go I." Facilitative self-disclosure is grace giving.

Secret 4: Get Out of the Spotlight

After you disclose, quickly refocus on the other person. A two- or three-sentence self-disclosure is usually more than adequate. Avoid the temptation to tell your life story and then to keep the spotlight firmly on yourself. Remember to quickly refocus on the other person's needs. Use the work sheet on page 105 to practice creating brief self-disclosure statements.

As you practice Christlike active listening, genuine proactive caring, asking great questions, and focused self-disclosure, you will notice two things. First, people thrive when you focus loving, respectful attention on them. As you practice true listening, they will begin to trust you and let you journey with them below the safe surface issues of their lives.

Second, they will invite you into some of their messy, confusing, and painful problems. They will begin looking to you for answers. This is the dangerous part of being quick to listen that we will address in the next chapter.

ENDNOTES

1. John Ortberg, *Everybody's Normal Till You Get to Know Them* (Grand Rapids, MI: Zondervan, 2003), 59.

2. Active wondering is an idea pioneered by our friend Doug Pollock, Cutting Edge Evangelism Director for Athletes in Action. Evangelistic applications of this technique are described in further detail in *Irresistible Evangelism: Natural Ways to Open Others to Jesus* by Steve Sjogren, Dave Ping, and Doug Pollock (Loveland, CO: Group Publishing, Inc., 2004).

▮▮▮ Self-Disclosure 101 ▮▮▮

This exercise assumes that you have a relationship with the person with whom you are talking and that you've already been listening with lots of warmth, empathy, and respect and will continue to do so. Read each situation, and ask yourself if you've experienced circumstances, feelings, or beliefs that clearly connect with the speaker's experience. Write them down. Then write a brief sentence that refocuses on the speaker.

1. My mother is eighty years old, and we're really concerned about the kind of meals she's eating.

Identify the speaker's belief, feeling, or experience:

Identify my own belief, feeling, or experience that is similar:

Refocus on the speaker:

2. I've been thinking about taking a new job in another state, but everyone in my family hates the idea of moving and leaving friends behind. I think it's the opportunity of a lifetime, but they think I'm just being selfish.

Identify the speaker's belief, feeling, or experience:

Identify my own belief, feeling, or experience that is similar:

Refocus on the speaker:

3. The speech therapist who has worked with our special-needs child for the last three years is taking family leave. I'm afraid we'll never find another therapist as good to replace her.

Identify the speaker's belief, feeling, or experience:

Identify my own belief, feeling, or experience that is similar:

Refocus on the speaker:

"It is a serious thing...to remember that the dullest...person you talk to may one day be a creature which...you would be strongly tempted to worship, or else a horror...such as you now meet...only in a nightmare. All day long we are...helping each other to one or other of these destinations."[1]

—C.S. Lewis

7

The "Dangers"
OF LISTENING

"**B**e afraid. Be very afraid." You may remember these words as the tag line from the 1986 remake of the movie *The Fly*, but they could just as easily apply to the aspects of listening leadership we are about to discuss. You don't believe it? What if we were to say "confrontation" or "speaking the truth in love" or "We need to talk about our relationship..."? Are you starting to feel at least a little bit scared? If you are, you're certainly not alone.

We've talked about being quick to listen and slow to speak; now it's time to talk about being *slow to anger*. The skills and attitudes we've discussed in earlier chapters help build trust and form strong relationships. But as every leader and every married person knows, there comes a time in every close relationship when the honeymoon is over. It's a time the foundation of caring, understanding, and respect we've built is tested by the day-to-day realities of competing needs and agendas. Although this stage of a relationship can get messy, it is nevertheless essential to the development of healthy, effective communities.

In his popular theory of group dynamics, education researcher Bruce Tuckman called this testing phase the *storm* stage.[2] *Storm* is a good description for this stage because this stage often includes interactions that can become loud, unsettling, or chaotic. In groups or individual relationships, storming behavior is characterized by a certain amount of defensiveness, anxiety, and outright opposition. Surprisingly, a reasonable amount of storming is necessary and beneficial in every kind of relationship. Yes, we said "beneficial."

> As people begin to feel more comfortable with us and trust that we won't reject them, they unconsciously begin to test the strength of our care for them by being honest. They may even deliberately say and do things to provoke us to anxiety and anger.

As people begin to feel more comfortable with us and trust that we won't reject them, they unconsciously begin to test the strength of our care for them by being honest. They may even deliberately say and do things to provoke us to anxiety and anger.

The storm can be a kind of "love test" that reveals how we will respond to people in the midst of stressful situations. Perhaps just as important, storms enable people to determine how we will allow them to treat us. The ways we choose to weather these critical relational storms will set the stage either for deeper commitment and cooperation or for insincere relationships and dysfunctional power struggles that could go on for years.

Patrick Lencioni, author of the best-selling business books *The Five Dysfunctions of a Team* and *Death by Meeting* says after lack of trust, avoidance of necessary conflict is one of the most damaging dysfunctions organizations and leaders ever face. Be sure to hear this: According to Lencioni, leaders who don't trust one another enough to engage in conflict are "incapable of engaging in unfiltered and passionate debate of ideas."[3]

Instead, Lencioni says, these leaders "resort to veiled discussions and guarded comments…Without having aired their opinions in the course of passionate and open debate, team members rarely, if ever, buy in and commit to decisions, though they may feign agreement."[4]

The Different Drum by M. Scott Peck brings this idea into a spiritual context, suggesting that if we do not allow for and navigate through the chaos stage, we end up with false community.[5] Many churches, not realizing the devastating outcome, opt to avoid or minimize conflict. On the surface, all is calm. But real life cannot flourish in false community. False community eventually leads to dead churches.

Even for those leaders who admit and embrace it, conflict is still a scary business. We've seen it destroy long-standing friendships, split congregations, and bring down whole ministries. In the face of chaos, there is good reason to be afraid and even *very afraid*.

Many if not most of us have not been equipped to handle the relational storms that inevitably come our way. Instead, like Jeff Goldblum's character in the movie *The Fly*, we feel the unhealthy force of our fallen humanity begin to take over in tense situations. We don't transform into disgusting giant insects, but we may feel our relationships mutating and taking on some of the destructive characteristics we discussed in Chapter 3. Our *natural* leadership prompts us to handle these stressful situations by becoming either reactive or passive.

In Ephesians 4:14-15, Paul suggests that our goal in stormy times might be "speaking the truth in love." Sadly, we often tend to separate truth and love in our relationships. We either reactively blast people with our version of the truth or passively make excuses for them in a weak parody of love. Let's look more closely at each of these unbalanced responses.

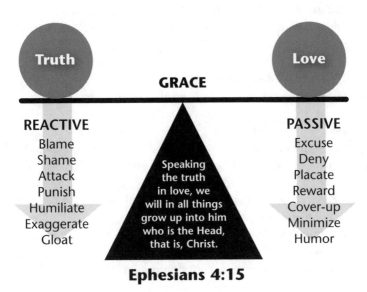

Truth

Love

GRACE

REACTIVE

Blame
Shame
Attack
Punish
Humiliate
Exaggerate
Gloat

Speaking the truth in love, we will in all things grow up into him who is the Head, that is, Christ.

PASSIVE

Excuse
Deny
Placate
Reward
Cover-up
Minimize
Humor

Ephesians 4:15

Unbalanced Believers

Overbalance toward reactive "truth-telling" creates a legalistic, almost Pharisaical mind-set. Remember the Pharisees who went after Jesus? Most of them were well-intentioned truth-tellers, but they didn't demonstrate much love or understanding. As the pendulum swings in this direction, we may at first find ourselves entertaining brief judgmental thoughts or adopting a slightly superior attitude toward a person who offends us. But soon, as James 1:13-15 tells us, these little attitudes conceive and give birth to bigger sins. Sarcastic words and bitter resentments emerge as we enforce our legalistic interpretations of how people should think and behave. We may begin to use blame and shame to scold people into compliance.

As the pendulum swings farther from love, we may engage in personal attacks, punitive behavior, and humiliation. We exaggerate others' faults and gloat over their disappointments. Finally, when these reactive sins are fully grown, they "give birth to death" (James 1:15). Spiritual death and relational death result when we fail to speak the truth in love.

Jesus spoke of this spiritual death in Matthew 5:21-22:

> You have heard that it was said to the people long ago, "Do not murder, and anyone who murders will be subject to judgment." But I tell you that anyone who is angry with his brother will be subject to judgment. Again, anyone who says to his brother, "Raca," is answerable to the Sanhedrin. But anyone who says, "You fool!" will be in danger of the fire of hell.

This is one of the scariest passages in the New Testament for anyone who has any tendency toward self-righteousness or even a mild temper. By this standard, we are all guilty and in need of forgiveness. We need help to think and act in more Christlike ways.

What happens when the pendulum swings the other way? What about those of us who, in love, gloss over the difficult task of truth-telling? We are in big trouble too. In some ways, this "loving avoidance" can create an even bigger relational storm because we are frequently unaware of the danger we are in.

At first we may lovingly (in our minds) look the other way as people do things that are harmful to themselves, to others, or to us. Without thinking, we become skilled at turning a blind eye to dishonest, unethical, or even criminal conduct. As the pendulum continues to swing, we become unwitting enablers of destructive and toxic acts we would never dream of committing ourselves. As Dr. Martin Luther King Jr. once said, "He who passively accepts evil is as much involved in it as he who helps to perpetrate it. He who accepts evil without protesting against it is really cooperating with it."[6]

Instead of confronting wrongdoing honestly and directly, we fall into a pattern of making excuses and denying the growing evidence we see and hear. Every night we may pray that the distressing insensitivity, abusiveness, or addiction we live with will go away, yet every day we continue to placate it, reward it, and cover up for it. As popular TV psychologist and best-selling author "Dr. Phil" McGraw regularly advises the parade of wounded people who choose to expose their personal problems on his national television show, "We teach people how to treat us."[7]

No matter what you may think of Dr. Phil and his media empire, this is one time he definitely has it right. We've seen it over and over. Women who are abused and employees who tolerate a culture of fear, dishonesty, and disrespect in the workplace have taught the husbands and bosses who victimize them exactly what they will and won't tolerate. They've been given a series of love tests and failed them all. In this case, they failed not by getting angry but by not loving others or respecting themselves enough to stand up and confront the storms as they happened.

Finding a Balance: Overcoming Our Fear of Confrontation

As Ralph Waldo Emerson once said, "The wise man in the storm prays God, not for safety from danger, but for deliverance from fear."[8] Speaking the truth in love can be a stormy proposition. We are wise to invite God to join us in this dangerous but important relational task. When God gave us free will, he knew we'd go through times of doubt and misunderstanding. God knew we might accept the gift but reject the Giver. But because God loved us so much, he must have decided the risk was worth it. As we work toward authentic relationships, friendships, and leadership, we, too, will have to take risks. We must overcome our fear of confrontation and begin to speak the truth in love.

When we ask our students what words come to mind when they hear the word *confrontation,* they usually respond with *fighting, anger, yelling, painful, run and hide,* and *avoid at all costs.* Clearly, many of their experiences have led them to fear and steer clear of situations that involve discussing disagreements or confronting unhealthy actions or attitudes. They are always surprised when we say, "Confrontation, done well, always expresses love." Love is the only motivation that is genuinely worth the risk.

> "Confrontation, done well, always expresses love." Love is the only motivation that is genuinely worth the risk.

Most motivations for confrontation do more harm than good. As we consider confrontation, we imagine the pleasure of telling off our boss or getting even with someone who hurt us. We visualize ourselves gleefully rubbing others' noses in the nasty behavior they've perpetrated against us and shouting, "See how it feels!" We salivate at the thought of proving the superiority of our ideas and exposing the foolishness of someone else's. It's natural to want to vindicate ourselves, but before we confront, we need to count the cost. Will we really feel vindicated if we've trampled on others in the process?

When our confrontation is motivated by vindication, it usually turns into a giant shouting match in which participants shout, "I'm right!" "No, you're not. I am!" "Are not!" "Are too!" or "I know you're not, but what am I?" Sounds childish, doesn't it? If this is what happens in confrontation, maybe we should avoid it! When we confront from motivations such as resentment, pride, envy, revenge, hatred, or selfish ambition, the consequences we reap are likely to hurt us as much or, in all likelihood, more than they hurt the people we want to get back at. So how do we confront in Christlike and genuinely helpful ways that balance love and truth?

Let's start by defining our terms. When we talk about Christlike confrontation, here's what we mean: *Christlike confrontation is a face-to-face meeting with someone we care about in which we point out apparent inconsistencies (1) between two or more things the person has said, (2) between something the person has said and something the person has done, (3) between what the person is reporting and other information you've been given, or (4) between the person's behavior and some external standard.* When we perceive these kinds of contradictions taking place around us, confrontation is usually in order. We choose to confront because not doing so gives a lie (from the enemy) a foothold in the life of someone we say we love.

Notice that this definition of confrontation is intended for situations in which there are perceived discrepancies between objective facts. It doesn't speak to the subjective emotions we may feel as a result. This is intentional. Feelings are elusive and personal, but facts are much easier to grasp and discuss. Later on we will learn how to handle the emotional dimension, but for now we'll stick to discussing the facts as we know them.

> We choose to confront because not doing so gives a lie (from the enemy) a foothold in the life of someone we say we love.

Using Confrontation to Make Sense of Apparent Contradictions

The first kind of inconsistency we mentioned (between two or more things someone has said) is usually the least threatening to confront. When confronting this type of inconsistency, you might say, "Last week you said you never wanted to talk to Julie ever again; now you're talking about hiring her as your personal assistant. Help me understand." In your mind, these two statements don't seem to go together, but you allow that there may be a reasonable explanation to clear up the contradiction. It's possible that the way Julie handled last week's misunderstanding really impressed the person you're talking with. As a result, now that person wants to hire her. This additional information makes sense of the apparent contradiction.

The second type of discrepancy (between a person's words and actions) is a bit more threatening but still fairly clear-cut. In this instance, you might say, "Jane, Tuesday you said you were going to get that publicity package to the graphic artist right away. It's Friday, and the package is still sitting on your desk. What's going on?" There may be (and you can start by assuming) a perfectly good reason why the package is still there. Maybe the graphic artist informed Jane that he or she would not be able to work on the publicity materials until Monday. Maybe Jane or another co-worker realized that the package was incomplete. Whatever the reason, you are justifiably asking Jane to provide some explanation for the delay. There is no need to raise your voice in an angry manner or lower it in apologetic tones; just use direct questions to get direct answers.

The third type of inconsistency (between what the person is reporting and other information you've been given) is a little more ominous. In this situation, you might say, "Marcus, I thought you assured me that our credit card account was completely paid off, but I just received a statement that says we carried over an unpaid balance of $3,000. Do you know why that might be?" This type of inconsistency must be handled carefully because the built-in implication is that somebody isn't telling the truth. But by inviting the person to explain, we can still leave the door open for other possible explanations, such as (in this situation) the check and the statement crossing in the mail.

The fourth possible discrepancy is between a person's behavior and some external standard. This one is difficult unless the standard is unambiguous and the person we are confronting subscribes to it. If you tell an unknown (to you) teenager puffing on a cigarette that he is "defiling the temple of the Holy Spirit," the gestures he will make are not likely to be gestures of repentance. On the other hand, we may successfully confront people we know by referring to known organizational policies or clearly articulated ethical and biblical standards.

In a case like this, you might say, "I see that your youth group is using pens with our company logo on them, but I don't recall that you asked us to donate them. Our policy is very specific about this kind of thing." This would no doubt be an uncomfortable, if not downright unpleasant, confrontation, and it would be tempting (and easier!) to look the other way. But remember, "speak the truth in love"! The biblical standard we need to confront *ourselves* with in these cases is found in Galatians 6:1: "Brothers, if someone is caught in a sin, you who are spiritual should restore him gently. But watch yourself, or you also may be tempted."

Steps to Christlike Confrontation

Before confronting anyone, do an honest personal inventory. Begin by identifying your fears (or anger or hurt) and earnestly praying about your motives. Do not confront unless you're reasonably sure that your motives are in the other person's best interest.

When Dave's wife, Pam, is considering Christlike confrontation, she always asks herself, "Am I doing this to get personal satisfaction, which explains my eagerness to 'correct' the other person, or is this an act of obedience, which usually comes with feelings of reluctance and requires lots of prayer before I'm willing to do what God wants me to do?"

After you've examined yourself and your motives, think about the things you'll say to the person you're confronting. There are three essential elements to a Christlike confrontation. They are similar to the essentials of Christlike active listening we learned in Chapter 5.

▋▋▋ Inviting

First, in a private conversation, invite the person you are confronting to consider the apparent contradiction you perceive. The words *invite* and *perceive* are important. Invitation is more respectful and far wiser than accusation or demand. It leaves room for choice. People can decline our invitation, but there may be consequences if they choose to do so. Also, our perceptions aren't always correct. When we confront, we genuinely hope that we will hear explanations that reconcile any seeming contradictions and correct any misperceptions we may have. We endeavor not to jump to conclusions or causes and not to prejudge the situation without first checking it out.

> When we confront, we genuinely hope that we will hear explanations that reconcile any seeming contradictions and correct any misperceptions we may have.

Depending on how immediate the need for resolution is and the depth of the relationship involved, you may want to begin with one of the following statements:

- ▋ "I'd like to talk to you about something I'm concerned about."

- ▋ "I wonder if you could take a few minutes to clear up something for me."

- ▋ "Can we get together after lunch to discuss something that's been on my mind?"

▋▋▋ Pointing Out Discrepancies

Second, concretely explain the apparent contradiction as matter-of-factly and dispassionately as possible. Address the specific actions, not the person's character or personality. There is a big difference between saying, "Marcus, didn't you assure me that our credit card account was completely paid off? I just received a statement that says we carried over an unpaid balance of $3,000," and "Marcus, you are such a liar!" or "Marcus, you are so irresponsible!"

As you confront, don't miss this important distinction! Actions can be changed and repented of, but character is permanent. In Matthew 7:1-2, Jesus says, "Do not judge, or you too will be judged. For in the same way you judge others, you will be judged, and with the measure you use, it will be measured to you." At first, Jesus' words may seem to contradict the exhortation to "gentle restoration" we read from Galatians 6:1. How can we restore others to right behavior without pointing out their sin?

Jesus' command not to judge refers not to behavior but to our unhealthy tendency to make negative judgments about people's nature or worth. When people make mistakes, they can make amends or change their ways. When we label others as liars or losers, we've weighed them and found them permanently wanting. As we understand Christ's teaching, any scarlet letter we pin on someone else will turn around and stick to our spirit where the true Judge of souls can see it.

Staying firmly and painstakingly in the realm of facts means acknowledging that our perceptions may be fallible. By sticking to the facts, we keep our tone neutral and help the other person do the same. That's why it doesn't hurt to precede our statements with tentative caveats such as

▪ "If my memory is correct..."

▪ "I could possibly be wrong, but..."

▪ "The way I remember our agreement is..."

▪ "It looks to me as though..."

Then, as simply and specifically as you are able, lay out the facts as you see them. Leave judgments and feelings out of it.

Do your best to speak in a neutral and nondefensive tone. Explain any seemingly contradictory words or actions in a way that helps the other person understand your concern without becoming overly defensive.

■■■ Inviting a Response

Third, calmly invite the other person to respond by offering his or her point of view about the discrepancies you've raised. Expect the person to be at least a little bit defensive, but do your best not to get hooked by this emotion. Understand that this is a natural response. (Think about how you'd feel if you were being confronted.) Set your defenses aside, and remember that how you handle this storm will determine the course of your future relationship—for good or ill. Keep in mind that your purposes are ultimately constructive and loving.

Use the Christlike active listening skills from Chapter 5 and proactive questions from Chapter 6 to help you manage the other person's responses. Instead of reacting to excuses or heated accusations, demonstrate empathy and understanding by tentatively reflecting the person's thoughts. Keeping your cool and keeping the spotlight on the other person's thoughts and feelings can often help de-escalate anxious or angry reactions.

You'll be surprised how quickly this straightforward approach works to handle most day-to-day confrontations. Instead of ignoring small discrepancies as no big deal, you can use these methods to confront them early, before they become big deals. That's what Hebrews 12:15 means when it says, "See to it that no one misses the grace of God and that no bitter root grows up to cause trouble and defile many."

When we confront with truth and love, people have an opportunity to experience grace. When we don't, little problems get buried and, like a hidden root of relational poison ivy, spring up to infect everyone who comes in contact with them. Soon the whole office, Sunday school class, or Board of Elders becomes irritable and itching to fight with you and with each other. Left unconfronted, even small interpersonal problems can destroy trust and lead whole organizations and churches into conflict. Remember Dave's tuna sandwich?

To learn to take the steps toward Christlike confrontation, take a few minutes to complete the exercise on page 126.

Positive Confrontation?

Confrontation doesn't have to be negative. In fact, if done properly, confrontation can lay a foundation for a new and improved understanding. This was our friend Lynne's experience. Lynne told us:

As a new member of my church's board of elders, I wasn't sure of the protocol or norms, so I spent the first few months observing. I noticed that people frequently left before the meeting was over. So one month I left quietly mid-meeting in order to make another appointment. The next evening I got a call from the moderator, who said, "I felt disrespected when you left early—not knowing if you were in disagreement with what we were discussing or what the reason for your departure was."

I apologized and explained my actions. This gave me an opportunity to ask what the procedure for early departure is. His immediate confrontation not only cleared the air of misunderstanding in our relationship but also pointed out the need for new members to get clear guidelines on expectations and protocol.

Defensive Responses

Confrontation can be difficult to initiate, but it's even harder to receive. And if you initiate it, you'd better be prepared to receive it as well. In spite of its negative connotation, confrontation plays a big part in keeping our relationships healthy. Think about the people who confront you most often. Aren't they also the people who love you most? And yet your first response to being confronted probably isn't "Thank you so much for helping me confront this problem in my life."

Even though we understand the need to speak the truth in love, we often respond to the people who confront us as if they're giving us grief. Actually *grief* is a fairly accurate word to describe how most people respond emotionally to being confronted. Elizabeth Kübler-Ross' famous five grief responses represent just a few of the emotional reactions we're likely to experience when we are confronted.[9]

■ *Denial:* "You must be mistaken; I never said or did anything of the sort."

■ *Anger:* "Who the #!&@/*? do you think you are, talking to me like that?"

■ *Bargaining:* "I'll admit that you're right if you'll admit you're being petty."

■ *Depression:* "I'm so messed up. My life is going nowhere..."

■ *Acceptance:* "I see what you are saying, and I agree we need to work this out."

We could add a few more responses of our own to Kübler-Ross' list.

■ *Victimization:* "When anything goes wrong, it's always my fault!"

■ *Manipulation:* "If you really cared about me, you'd let this go."

■ *Stonewalling:* "I'm really not interested in anything you might have to say."

We need not be shocked when we encounter any or all of these reactions as we confront and as we are confronted ourselves. Instead, we need to practice a little more of the fruit of the Spirit in these moments. We can give grace by offering respect, staying friendly with our tone as well as our words, and consciously choosing not to get defensive. Most of all, we give grace simply by truly listening.

Whew! This listening business is a lot harder than you thought it was going to be. But if you work at it diligently, you'll eventually find joy in doing it. Huh? Unless you are a little strange, the storms and trials we've been talking about probably don't make you want to jump for joy—at least not until they're over and the air is clear again. However, James 1:2-3 tells us to "consider it pure joy, my brothers, whenever you face trials of many kinds, because you know that the testing of your faith develops perseverance." True listening can test your faith, and it definitely requires perseverance. Because after the seeking, the asking, the wondering, and the Christlike confrontation, you're still not finished. Someone has to clear the air, and, quick-to-listen leader, that someone is usually you.

Clearing the Air—The Skill of Immediacy

Clearing the air means going beyond the facts brought to light in the confrontation and dealing with how we feel toward one another. It's taking proactive steps to heal any lingering emotional tension or wounds. This is very important because how we handle emotional tests and storms will determine the norms of what's acceptable in the relationship and how well we will perform and cooperate together in future interactions.

The name psychologists have given to the process of working out the emotional kinks in our relationships is *immediacy*. The word, as you might guess, comes from the word *immediate*, and that's part of what it means. When there's emotional maintenance work to be done, we don't pass "Go," we don't collect $200; we deal with it *immediately.*

The word *immediately* is used over forty-six times in the New Testament, mostly when Jesus is performing miraculous healings. When Jesus saw a need, he didn't mess around; he went to work healing and restoring health without delay. When he saw tension and fear in his disciples as he walked to them on the water, "Immediately he spoke to them and said, 'Take courage! It is I. Don't be afraid' " (Mark 6:50).

> Christ-centered immediacy means stopping what we are doing right now and taking all the steps in our power to heal and restore whatever may be wrong in our relationships.

When we talk about being immediate with people, we mean proactively doing what Jesus would do if he were in our place in that moment. We're talking not about the WWJD slogan that was printed on so many T-shirts and Bible covers a few years back but about the real thing. Christ-centered immediacy means stopping what we are doing right now and taking all the steps in our power to heal and restore whatever may be wrong in our relationships.

You may need to work through the feelings that came out after you confronted someone or were confronted. You may need to confess a mistake and ask forgiveness. Maybe you have a nagging feeling that there is still something unresolved in the relationship. Or you might feel the prompting of the Holy Spirit to connect with and encourage someone.

It's a little scary to take the initiative to seek out others and to do what's in your power to work things out, but it's worth it. As the saying goes, "What's not worked out will eventually be acted out." Today's unresolved problems and unfinished emotional business have within them the seeds of tomorrow's divorce, next month's congregational split, and next year's devastating sexual misconduct. If we take immediate action to deal with problems before they take root, we will spare ourselves and our loved ones tremendous heartache.

The secretary at Lynne's Rotary Club left office with three months remaining in her term. Then, Lynne explains:

The club members asked me if I would fill in for her until elections. I confessed I was not a detail-oriented person and didn't think I was a good replacement but would try to help if they couldn't find someone more suited to fill the gap. They asked me to take on the secretarial duties.

One of those duties was to create name badges for new members. This had totally slipped my mind until I noticed several new members had badges. Someone had taken care of it for me. Not knowing who had done this task or who might be covering other jobs I was missing, I started to feel uncomfortable and very guilty about my poor job performance. At first I couldn't look other members in the eye, and eventually I stopped attending.

After missing a few meetings, I realized I needed to be immediate and asked to be put on the next meeting agenda. I explained how guilty I was feeling after seeing some of my tasks being anonymously taken care of and that, although this was meant to be a kind gesture, I was feeling confused and ultimately disrespected by the lack of direct communication. I encouraged them to be honest with me so I could improve and grow rather than continue to feel inadequate and inferior.

I find myself seeking out relationships with people who love me enough to be honest and hold me accountable so I can grow. People who are willing to confront me have become a very important reflection of how God loves me.

Once you've made up your mind to be immediate, go quickly. As Jesus taught in Matthew 5:23-24, "If you are offering your gift at the altar and there remember that your brother has something against you, leave your gift there in front of the altar. First go and be reconciled to your brother; then come and offer your gift." Apparently, there is no act of worship or service to God that is more important than reconciliation, or immediacy as we've referred to it here.

In his book *Everybody's Normal Till You Get to Know Them*, John Ortberg describes a phrase he's introduced into every church in which he has served. The phrase goes like this: "We need to have a little 'Matthew 18:15' conversation." Ortberg points out seven immediate steps inherent in what Christ teaches in this verse. These seven steps are about as uncomplicated as they could be, even if they're not always easy.

1. When there is an interpersonal problem

2. You

3. Go

4. To the person

5. In private

6. And discuss it

7. For the purpose of restoring relationship [10]

"When there is an interpersonal problem"—Step one requires us to get out of denial. Notice it doesn't say "if" there are interpersonal problems but "when." We do ourselves and others a grave disservice when we turn a blind eye to our elephant-size problems and say, "Everything's just fine between us." One definition of denial we've heard makes a suitable acrostic from the word:

Don't

Even

kNow

I

Am

Lying

Ask the Lord to show you if there is anyone with whom you need to work out a problem. If you're feeling brave, set this book aside and do it right now.

When we're in denial, we don't even know we're lying to ourselves or to others. Fortunately, part of the Holy Spirit's job in our lives is to convict us of sin and lead us toward righteousness. When in doubt, just ask the Lord to show you if there is anyone with whom you need to work out a problem. If you're feeling brave, set this book aside and do it right now. You'll find that God is very faithful in bringing folks to mind.

"You"—Step two in the immediacy process is "you." Don't wait around for the person who has hurt

you to show up on your doorstep. You'll be waiting a long time—too long. And the person you think you may have wounded? That person may be too hurt to come to you. So go to him or her. Immediacy is about "owning" your stuff and taking responsibility for your own thoughts, feelings, and actions. It's about being proactive.

"Go"—In step three, *go* means go. No more avoiding, no more putting it off till the right moment; today is the day. Get prayed up and calmed down, and go speak to the person now. If you've been procrastinating, put it on your calendar and make an appointment. Make a phone call to set it up, but don't try to do it over the phone if you can find any other way. Face to face is the most powerful way to clear the air. Remember, body language will help communicate that you care when words are lacking.

"To the person"—Step four directs *you* (2) to *go* (3) *to the person* (4). When we have a problem with someone, why is it so much easier to talk to everyone but him or her about it? Proverbs 26:20 says, "Without wood a fire goes out; without gossip a quarrel dies down." In all but the most difficult cases, going to others instead of the person directly involved is like pouring gasoline on a lit bonfire. It's dangerous, and lots of people are likely to get hurt. "Holy gossip" is probably the most destructive kind. We can't imagine many things more offensive to God's ears than prayer requests offered on behalf of others that start out "Don't tell anyone; we need to pray for Charlie…and you'll never guess why!" It's best to leave third parties out of it unless you've tried a direct face-to-face approach and it hasn't worked. If this is the case, then, following Matthew 18:16, you might call in one or two Christian mediators to help.

> When we have a problem with someone, why is it so much easier to talk to everyone but him or her about it?

"In private"—Step five seems pretty obvious, but many Christians cling to the notion that there is strength in numbers. Trust us when we say this: Most people will not respond well to being publicly put on the spot. Private is almost always better. If in doubt, ask yourself, "If I had a problem, how and where would I want a loving confrontation to take place?"[11]

"Discuss it"—In step six, *discuss* means having a thorough, two-way dialogue in which you do your best to speak your piece, then listen to the other person warmly, respectfully, and with your best Christlike active listening skills. As you discuss the situation, avoid

the temptation to try to fix things before you've built a clear under-standing of what both of you are thinking and feeling. Often you will find that the problem you thought was the problem is not the prob-lem. Until the underlying issues are on the table, it's almost impossi-ble to make real headway. Depending on the problem, listening might take anywhere from thirty minutes to several hours spread out over several sessions. This may seem like a long time, but a few hours of work is usually well worth the investment if it prevents bitterness from taking root.

"For the purpose of restoring relationship"—Step seven is the reason we got together in the first place: We want to clear the air and restore relationship. We want to accomplish God's purposes in God's way.

Every close working relationship, friendship, and marriage requires frequent immediacy pit stops. Smart leaders are like good race car drivers because they know that the harder and faster they drive, the more essential it is to pull into the pit to make sure every-thing's operating properly. Now take a few minutes to complete the work sheet on pages 127 and 128.

Now that you've considered guidelines for skillfully keeping rela-tionships clean and healthy through loving confrontation and imme-diacy, you're ready to help protect your successes from relational sabotage by

1. recognizing and dealing with communication barriers and

2. recognizing and dealing with the strengths and limitations of your leadership temperament and listening style.

We will deal with these topics in Chapter 8.

ENDNOTES

1. C.S. Lewis, *The Weight of Glory: And Other Addresses* (New York, NY: HarperCollins, 1976), 45-46.

2. Bruce W. Tuckman, *Developmental Sequence in Small Groups* (Psychological Bulletin, American Psychological Association, Volume 63, Number 6, 1965), 384-399. As leaders we are often concerned about the development of the vari-ous groups with which we work. Frequently we make reference to "the stages of group development," and the stages we cite most often are forming, storm-ing, norming, and performing. Originally proposed by Bruce Tuckman in 1965, these stages were based on his examination of empirical research studies. In this classic article, we find a rich description of these stages under a variety of settings as well as their applicability to both group structure and task activity.

3. Patrick Lencioni, *The Five Dysfunctions of a Team: A Leadership Fable* (San Francisco, CA: Jossey-Bass, 2002), 188.

4. Ibid., 188-189.

5. M. Scott Peck, *The Different Drum: Community-Making and Peace* (New York, NY: Simon and Schuster, 1987), 86-90.

6. *The International Thesaurus of Quotations* (New York, NY: HarperCollins, 1996), 202.

7. Phillip C. McGraw, *Life Strategies: Doing What Works, Doing What Matters* (New York, NY: Hyperion, 1999).

8. *The International Thesaurus of Quotations*, 139.

9. Elizabeth Kübler-Ross, *On Death and Dying* (New York, NY: Macmillan Publishing Co., Inc., 1969).

10. John Ortberg, *Everybody's Normal Till You Get to Know Them* (Grand Rapids, MI: Zondervan, 2003), 130. Our steps are slightly different from John's.

11. There are some serious privacy considerations here related to being inappropriately alone with members of the opposite sex or with people who have previously proven so hostile and untrustworthy that witnesses are required. Most churches and organizations have good policies and guidelines about what's fitting and proper and what's not.

▮▮▮ Learning to Confront ▮▮▮

1. A staff member says everything is fine; she loves her job, and she has just become engaged. However, you notice that she hardly ever smiles, and she doesn't want to talk about any of her wedding plans.

Tentative opening:

Discrepancy:

Invite response:

2. A church member says he wants to get more involved in church activities, but you have often heard him turn down leaders who've invited him to participate.

Tentative opening:

Discrepancy:

Invite response:

3. A Christian contractor from your fellowship agreed to paint your elderly parents' kitchen over three weeks ago. He has not followed through on that commitment.

Tentative opening:

Discrepancy:

Invite response:

▮▮▮ Immediacy Practice ▮▮▮

Using the following situations, imagine how you would invite the following people to talk over the dynamics of your relationship.

1. A key leader and longtime friend from your church seems distant. Several times you've both been at gatherings, and your friend seems to be avoiding you.

Describe the situation. Be as concrete, specific, and accurate as possible.

Using "I" statements, describe your perceptions.

Encourage the other person to share his or her thoughts and feelings about what is going on in the relationship.

2. A staff member you have known and liked for years has been showing up late for work for the last few weeks, missing important meetings, and dismissing the suggestions of fellow team members in unusually harsh ways.

Describe the situation. Be as concrete, specific, and accurate as possible.

Using "I" statements, describe your perceptions.

Encourage the other person to share his or her thoughts and feelings about what is going on in the relationship.

3. You have heard from three different sources that a trusted volunteer leader you've been supervising is spreading malicious rumors about church staff members. This person has not come to you or any of the staff members in question with any concerns. This behavior seems very out of character from what you know of this person.

Describe the situation. Be as concrete, specific, and accurate as possible.

Using "I" statements, describe your perceptions.

Encourage the other person to share his or her thoughts and feelings about what is going on in the relationship.

*"Not many of you should presume to be teachers, my broth-
ers, because you know that we who teach will be
judged more strictly" (James 3:1).*

*"This year, or this month, or, more likely, this very
day, we have failed to practise ourselves the kind of
behaviour we expect from other people."[1]*
—C.S. Lewis

8

Breaking the ~~Sound~~
LISTENING BARRIER(S)

B eing human is frustrating. It's been twelve years since we co-
authored our first book about listening and started being introduced as "listening experts." Ever since, our lives have been
filled with humbling examples of how far we fall short of what we
know and teach. Our spouses regularly reprove us both, saying,
"Now might be a good time for some of that listening stuff you teach!"
Friends and co-workers constantly catch us being inattentive or talking too much. It's almost (but not quite) humorous how many times
we find ourselves saying, "I just teach about listening, but I'm not
always good at it." Like being married and having children, teaching
and leading others is a superb way to have all of your faults exposed
and highlighted on a regular basis.

Being a leader is frustrating. Like all humans, leaders have barriers to overcome as we seek to become quick to listen. But because
we've chosen to focus our attention on leading others, we may be

blind to the barriers that are within us. We need others to help us see clearly by speaking the truth in love. See if any of the following five barriers seem familiar to you.

Breaking the Perfection Barrier

Leaders should be perfect listeners, right? Wrong! As much as we wish it were not so, leaders are just as riddled with shortcomings as everyone else. The only big difference between leaders and our followers is that for the benefit of the body of Christ, we've answered the call to "walk our talk" in front of others.

In his outstanding book *Empowered Church Leadership*, Brian J. Dodd explains that since medieval times leaders in the church have been encouraged to behave as performers and their followers as spectators. This isn't very respectful from either vantage point. Dodd says:

> The only big difference between leaders and our followers is that for the benefit of the body of Christ, we've answered the call to "walk our talk" in front of others.

The pastor is the trained lecturer, and the congregants are supposed to be good listeners and put their money in the offering plate. In some ways this academic/spectator model is a reflection of the seminaries that have trained the pastors.[2]

Thrust into this academic/performer role, many leaders attempt to avoid the humiliation of having their flaws exposed by shaping an "ideal persona" of the impressive leader they would like to be. We all do this from time to time. Our good works don't look good enough, so, like actresses or actors, we begin "improving" on them and carefully applying makeup to cover our flaws.

Even though we may not like it, we get caught up in playing this role because it's what's expected of us or because it's what our followers or some of the influential players in our organization seem to demand. We let concerns about image, appearance, and public relations shape how we listen and relate to those around us.

Jesus was and is well aware of our tendency to embellish genuinely good works to make ourselves appear more impressive. *The Message* version of Matthew 6:1-4 puts it this way:

> *Be especially careful when you are trying to be good so that you don't make a performance out of it. It might be good*

theater, but the God who made you won't be applauding.

When you do something for someone else, don't call attention to yourself. You've seen them in action, I'm sure— "playactors" I call them—treating prayer meeting and street corner alike as a stage, acting compassionate as long as someone is watching, playing to the crowds. They get applause, true, but that's all they get. When you help someone out, don't think about how it looks. Just do it—quietly and unobtrusively. That is the way your God, who conceived you in love, working behind the scenes, helps you out.

When we call attention to or exaggerate our impressive works, Jesus calls us *hypocrites* in the classical Greek theater sense of the word. In Christ's time, a hypocrite was an actor who wore a stereotypical mask. We've all seen the grinning mask that represents comedy and the gloomy mask that represents tragedy. Unfortunately, we're also all too familiar with the kind of mask that Jesus spoke of in the passage above. It's a mask that's easy for leaders to put on and hard for them to take off. It portrays a tepid "be warmed and comforted" brand of compassion that is designed for show. Though most of us can see right through this facade in others, we catch ourselves acting it out in our leadership roles.

Why do we do this? Brian Dodd suggests that many Christian leaders learn these habits from the people who train them. It may not be part of the official curriculum, but leaders in training pick it up by reading between the lines as they watch eminent instructors and leadership role models handle their followers' expectations. Dodd argues that this "hidden curriculum" perpetuates a kind of leader who is ineffective at the relationships that are most important. He says, "They may feel comfortable in their study, at committee meetings and leading worship services, but they readily feel out of their depth in sharing Jesus with a not-yet Christian who is their next-door neighbor."[3]

Our purpose here is not to point fingers but to challenge ourselves to recognize that one of our best advantages is the fact that we aren't the smarter, older brothers sent to lead the hurting, lost, and lonely. In all the most important ways, *we are them*. We are human. We struggle. We fail, and though we may have learned a lot, we haven't figured out all the answers or even how to consistently apply the ones we do have. By ourselves, we don't have much to offer. But where our limited competency, wisdom, and skills end, God's unlimited sufficiency, understanding, and power begin.

Three Choices

In their book *The Lessons of Experience: How Successful Executives Develop on the Job,* Morgan McCall Jr., Michael Lombardo, and Ann Morrison put forward three basic choices anyone who wants to grow as a leader must make.[4]

The first choice is to recognize your shortcomings and identify areas in which there is room for improvement. Whether you like it or not, sooner or later you will be forced to confront your weaknesses. They will eventually come out one way or another. You can either try to avoid your deficiencies and wait around for some catastrophic event to reveal them or actively jump into situations that provide feedback to help you grow and stretch your skills. This is the way we've successfully managed to teach tens of thousands of leaders how to listen more effectively: We put them in situations in which they actually have to practice the theories they've learned, then we give them immediate and honest feedback about what they are doing well and how they need to improve.

The second choice we must face as leaders is whether to accept responsibility for our shortcomings. If we deny our shortcomings, we are choosing not to grow past them. When we attempt to deny our shortcomings, we may shift blame to others or avoid situations in which our flaws might be revealed. Denial might temporarily maintain the perfection facade, but instead of remediating our flaws, it perpetuates them. Only by accepting our shortcomings can we identify and work on improving in these areas. Our students often tell us that they never realized what poor listeners they were or what they could do about it until they attended one of our workshops. Accepting that you need to improve is the first giant step toward improvement.

The third choice we all have to make is what to do about our weaknesses once they come to light. You've read several chapters on how to become a more Christlike active listener and confronter. If all you do is read without challenging yourself, putting what you learned into practice, and getting honest feedback from others on your progress, you may actually be worse off than before. You may be at risk of confusing *knowing* something about listening with *doing* it. In this case, knowledge separated from experience is worse than useless; it's dangerous.

Falling into the trap of thinking, "I know all about this listening stuff" is a lot like saying, "I know all about soap." There is no benefit to *knowing about* it unless you strip off your old clothes, get wet, and go to work scrubbing away. The real benefit to both soap and listening comes only as you learn to apply them consistently. Occasional use on special occasions just won't cut it.

> The real benefit to both soap and listening comes only as you learn to apply them consistently. Occasional use on special occasions just won't cut it.

Breaking the perfection barrier and letting people see our imperfections as we work on them takes real courage. Some of our followers would rather we keep up our "holier than thou" appearance than face the reality that we're just as imperfect and in need of God's grace as they are. They will resist and oppose the honesty and vulnerability that come as we lay aside false pretenses. Many more will welcome and bless any leader who is willing to do so. They're just as tired of shallow religion as we are. They're hungry for real relationships with real people who know a real God. They are ready to follow someone authentic and honest enough to show the way by working on their own rough edges.

In John 8:32, Jesus proclaims that we will know the truth, and the truth will set us free! The New Testament word John uses to describe the truth in this verse is *aletheia*. It means to pull back the veil and to reveal the *true truth* or the *real reality*. A willingness to be real ourselves and to offer others safe places where they can be heard is the beginning of the quick-to-listen community we talked about in Chapter 2.

Breaking the Impatience Barrier

Faced with a long line at the supermarket or video store, have you ever gotten so fed up that you just groaned in despair, turned around, and stomped off in disgust without getting what you came for? Have you ever moaned inwardly when the friends you invited to dinner stayed and talked and chatted on and on...long after you'd lost interest? Has your spouse, child, or a co-worker ever ambushed you as you came in the door and then poured out an endless sob story about how badly his or her day has been going? Have you ever sat in a committee meeting where a well-meaning but anal-retentive officer ground agonizingly through hundreds of extraneous details on the way to some obscure point you couldn't care less about?

These word pictures are probably not what come to mind when you think of the passage in Romans 8:22 that talks about the "whole creation" groaning inwardly "right up to the present time." That *is* the way it feels, though. It's as if all of creation is standing with us near the end of that practically endless line or waiting eagerly for that long-winded conversation to get to the point. In situations like these, impatience is natural and understandable but, as a Christlike response, not acceptable. Instead, we need to deal with the frustration we're feeling and will continue to feel until God finishes the redemptive work he's started in us. Meanwhile, we can pray for more patience—one of the supernatural fruits of the Spirit listed in Galatians 5:22-23.

The King James Version of the Bible uses the word *longsuffering* to describe this ability to endure waiting without becoming upset and to persevere calmly while facing difficulty. Patience also involves the capacity to extend grace and endure irritation, hurt, or even provocation without losing your temper. Patience is a virtue, but for most of us, it doesn't come naturally. As we struggle with impatience, it's tempting to let poor anger management become one of those human failings we share with our followers. After all, they want us to be real, right? And real people get angry.

This approach might be honest, and it might even feel good at the time, but it rarely, if ever, builds up the body of Christ. In their book *The Leadership Lessons of Jesus*, television producer Bob Briner and pastor Ray Pritchard speak of leaders who extol impatience and insensitivity as virtues.

"The hard-nosed, knock-the-walls-down, slash-and-burn, victory-at-any-price kind of leadership always has its proponents; this kind of leader is often lauded—for a while. However, enduring leadership, the kind that makes a positive, long-range difference, is always characterized by compassion."[5]

That's just it; listening takes patience and *real* compassion. It calls on us to overcome that which is uncharitable, irritable, indifferent, and sarcastic in our fallen human nature. The kind of listening we're talking about requires real discipline and mental energy—not to keep up but to slow down and concentrate on what others are saying. It takes our undivided attention. Most people can comprehend well over 300 words per minute, but the average person speaks at a rate of 125 to 175 words per minute. All the while, we are thinking at ten times that speed. As all these things are going on, there are lots of ways to get mentally sidetracked or distracted.

In Colossians 3:12, Paul recognizes that we all have unkind inclinations from time to time. He struggled with them himself. That's why Paul advises us to "clothe" ourselves "with compassion, kindness, humility, gentleness and patience." In other words, we must be quick to listen even when it is the last thing our flesh wants to do. This is the sign of a true leader. As we work to develop patience, others will follow our lead. Over time, as we grow in patience, an atmosphere of Christlike calm will come to characterize our environment. And with patience will come grace for the times we inevitably fall short of our desire to model Jesus.

Breaking the Distraction Barrier

So what about all those distractions? We live in a distracting and distractible world. According to Bob Lerer, a pediatrician we know, attention-deficit disorder (ADD) and attention-deficit (hyperactivity) disorder (ADHD) are estimated to affect anywhere from 3 to 10 percent of school-age children in America. Students with ADD or ADHD demonstrate great difficulty maintaining focus on their schoolwork and usually have a hard time concentrating on important tasks long enough to complete them. The good news is that 70 to 80 percent of those who suffer from these problems respond well to medication, changes in diet, or other treatments. The bad news for those reading this book is that *100 percent* of Christian leaders, all of our followers, and, for that matter, all human beings, suffer from what pastor John Ortberg calls *"spiritual* attention deficit disorder."[6]

No matter what our particular leadership temperament may be, we are all easily distracted from the things that matter most to God. The children of Israel constantly lost track of what God was telling them in the wilderness. Jesus' disciples were distracted from listening to the Word of God incarnate by their own infighting as they argued over who was greatest. We are no different. Like those who've come before, we, too, have a chronically difficult time attending to "our father's business."

Spiritual ADD and spiritual ADHD (attention-deficit *hypocrisy* disorder) can cause us to lose track of what's eternal and important in the haze of the conflicting internal and external "noise" around us. Just as attention-deficit disorder prevents many students from performing well in school, spiritual ADD keeps us from living up to our potential as leaders in the body of Christ. Unfortunately, there is no medication or sugar-free diet that will cure us. The only effective treatment we've found is developing and practicing a spiritual discipline we call *listening for heaven's sake.*

We all have our own reasons for listening or not listening. We might listen to people if we think what they're saying is interesting. We'll listen if listening will reward us with something we want or help us avoid something we don't want. This is *listening for the sake of self-interest.* No one has to write a book on listening for self-interest's sake because nearly everyone listens this way naturally. If you were to overhear a conversation between two pirates as one gave directions to where his fortune in gold was buried, nobody would have to tell you to listen. That conversation would instantly get your undivided attention!

New parents with a sick baby don't have to be told to listen intently to every tiny sound coming from the crib or baby monitor. Without prompting, they constantly check and recheck the things they hear. This is *listening for anxiety's sake.* The greater the anxiety, the more intently the parents will pay attention. By the second or third child, anxiety over childhood illness diminishes, and the parents tune in only intermittently. Expensive baby monitors disappear onto unreachable shelves or to the darkest recesses of the bedroom closet. Familiarity eventually overcomes anxiety, and it becomes easier and easier not to listen.

Listening for love's sake is something we've all either seen or experienced. When we are infatuated or in love, we don't need to be reminded to listen to our beloved. If you look around any restaurant or public place, you can usually gauge how long the couples there have been together. The newly smitten and newly married stand out because they are so intent on each other. They respond to their partners' every move and gesture. The old married couples, on the other hand, are looking and talking in every direction but where their spouses are sitting. As time passes even the most loving couples develop a kind of immunity to the volatile mix of hormones, pheromones, and romantic magic that attracted them in the first place.

No matter how powerful the initial attraction—whether it's based on self-interest, anxiety, or love—we eventually get distracted. Our intentions may be the very best, but our flesh fights good listening every inch of the way. Legions of inner anxieties and competing agendas battle for our attention.

For Christian leaders, avoiding distraction may be doubly or triply difficult. Our various agendas and organizational visions loom large. We are balancing tight schedules filled with important appointments and critical decisions that pull our focus away from the person's story we have been called to listen to at the moment. We look at our watches and fidget in our seats. We formulate clever responses and impressive advice that will make us appear wise in the speaker's eyes. In the process, we lose track of what people are saying and waste some of our most powerful opportunities to serve those God has called us to lead.

According to Laurie Beth Jones, author of *Jesus, CEO*, "Focus is one of the key attributes of a leader, and nowhere is it more powerful when applied to and on behalf of another human being." When we focus, we *behold* the person sitting before us as Jesus would, Jones explains. "There is long and direct eye contact, and the leader focuses concentration on that person so that she or he feels like the most important person in the room."[7]

Henri Nouwen also gives a picture of the power of listening when he says:

> *Listening is much more than allowing another to talk while waiting for a chance to respond. Listening is paying full attention to others and welcoming them into our very beings. The beauty of listening is that those who are listened to start feeling accepted, start taking their words more seriously and discovering their true selves.*[8]

Although we may be tempted to smile and make light of our spiritual ADD, it's not really a laughing matter. When the people we serve are in pain...or in love...or trying to figure out the direction of their lives, they want and need our full attention. Since God has come to dwell in the hearts of ordinary men and women, when we are listening, we are often treading on hallowed ground. It's a holy place that requires us to remove our shoes and leave behind any distractions that don't belong there.

Breaking the Preconception Barrier

If you've been a leader for long, you've probably heard a few stories and complaints from different people that sound an awful lot alike. As we hear these seemingly similar accounts, we're reminded of Paul's teaching in 1 Corinthians 10:13 that "no temptation has seized you except what is common to man." On the surface, this teaching seems to indicate that all human problems and our responses to them will tend to follow fairly predictable patterns. So it's only natural that when we are listening to a person's story and it starts to sound like something we've heard or experienced before, we tend to jump to conclusions. Using our previous experiences and our fertile imaginations, we fill in the blanks of what hasn't been said. Like radio commentator Paul Harvey, we're pretty sure we already know "the rest of the story."

One time Anne returned home after a weekend of teaching listening skills to find one of her teenage daughters sitting calmly in the family room.

> I'd noticed that the family car my daughter had been driving was missing from our garage. I was sure she'd driven it or loaned it to one of her reckless friends without my permission. I was already working out punishments and delivering angry lectures about negligence and irresponsibility in my head. She had no inkling of the storm of righteous indignation about to be unleashed upon her as I brusquely barked, "Where's the car?"
>
> My daughter just looked at the crazy woman I was quickly becoming and calmly replied, "Dad took it out to fill it up with gas for me." The conclusions I'd jumped to evaporated into an audible and exasperated sigh. I sat down and gave my now completely mystified daughter a huge hug. Anyone who has teenagers at home knows how close I'd come to igniting a major incident in our household. Even though I know better and have taught thousands of others how to do better, there have been many other times I didn't slow down and stop to listen before going off like a misguided missile.

Leaders and parents alike often believe we know exactly what's going on in the minds of our followers (or children). It's amazing how very wrong and destructive our conclusions can be. Dave tells a story to illustrate.

> *I was driving into the parking lot of our ministry's office after a lunch appointment. As I parked my car, I noticed one of our board members heading out the door in an obviously distraught state. I intercepted her on the way to her car and asked what was the matter. For the next forty-five minutes, I stood next to her car as she furiously poured her hurt and anger about how disrespectfully she felt she had just been treated by one of my senior staff members. From what I could discern, the staff person in question had called this influential board member "haughty."*
>
> *Even though I couldn't imagine the staff person speaking to her that way, I promised the board member I would talk to this person and take appropriate disciplinary action. As you might imagine, I was not very pleased with what I'd been hearing. So I went directly to that staff person's office and asked for an explanation of what had taken place between her and the board member. The staff person's story was a revelation.*
>
> *As they'd been working on our ministry fund-raising banquet together, the staff person had tried to connect on a more friendly level with the board member by complimenting her appearance. In what may have been a somewhat overly familiar and joking manner, she'd said, "Has anyone told you that you're a real hottie?" In slang terms, the staff member had been trying to tell her that her outfit looked very stylish or sexy. Completely unfamiliar with the slang term, what the board member heard was "Has anyone ever told you you're really haughty?" Ouch! It's not hard to see why she'd felt so attacked and disrespected. Neither of the two women understood what had happened to them, and both were hurt and offended.*
>
> *If I hadn't taken the time to slow down all the jumping to conclusions, this misunderstanding might have cost our ministry two of its most important team members. Although I was more than a little tempted to join in the confusion by jumping to my own conclusions, I forced myself to set aside*

my preconceptions and use listening to get to the bottom of things. This is one time being quick to listen turned a potential tragedy into something we can all look back on and laugh at now.

Another preconception problem is "jumping to causes." This happens when we assume we know what's motivating another person to react a certain way without bothering to ask or listen. When we jump to a cause, we assume a judgmental or superior role and project hidden, ulterior motives onto someone else's behavior. In a leadership context, we might assume if an employee of a minority race is having problems fitting in, it's because he has a chip on his shoulder. In this instance the not-so-nice word for jumping to cause would be *prejudice*. Prejudice is not just a racial problem; it's an attitude we demonstrate all the time. If we've ever prejudged what makes someone else tick, without getting our answers directly from the person, we're guilty.

As odd as it may seem, breaking through the preconception barriers means replacing all our old presumptions and presuppositions with a single new one. Instead of presuming to know what happened (jumping to conclusions) or why it happened (jumping to causes), we will presume only that *we don't yet understand*. We will take for granted that only God is omniscient and only he has the ability to read the future and the hearts of men and women. God chose not to give us the gift of omniscience (and aren't we glad!), but he did give us the humble but powerful ability to listen to the people around us. It's a gift that only works at very close range. So instead of speeding ahead to where we think people might be going or sneaking around behind them to unearth the buried causes that have shaped their choices, *we can meet them where they are* and walk with them.

Breaking the Fear Barrier

Revelation always seems to be surrounded by fear. Have you noticed that when angels appear in Scripture, the first words they usually say are "Fear not!" The alarm Abraham and Daniel and Mary and Joseph all experienced could be attributed to the shock of confronting a dazzling supernatural being. There is also probably something more to it. When angels showed up with a revelation from God, any illusions of control over a tidy, self-contained world burst like flimsy soap bubbles. When angels show up, the truth they reveal can be awe-ful. Truth that is bigger than us or beyond our control is unsettling and even terrifying.

So what does this have to do with listening? Are we saying that every person we listen to carries a potential revelation that could burst our bubble of self-sufficiency or self-control? In a word, yes. Listening is an intrinsically scary business that forces us out of our comfort zones into awe-ful places to which we'd rather not go.

As leaders who listen, what we'll hear, more often than not, is criticism. This comes with the territory of talking God's talk and trying to walk his walk in front of others. It's no fun to be the target of other people's "constructive" analysis and critical judgment. Being human, our natural tendency is to defend ourselves by attacking, by pretending this doesn't bother us, by avoiding it, or by becoming pouting, emotional victims. We may not even be conscious that we are doing any of these things, but the people around us are.

> Listening is an intrinsically scary business that forces us out of our comfort zones into awe-ful places to which we'd rather not go.

Anne explains what happens when she becomes defensive:

> *I believe that I am trapped. I have dug a hole for myself, and I am not going to get out. Frantically, I try every possible way to escape the situation while still trying to save face. I try to protect myself from looking stupid or being embarrassed and, in the process, actually begin to look more brainless and rattled than before. If we could only step out of our bodies and see ourselves at one of these moments, we would probably be close to finding the cure.*

If you're not sure what you do or how you look when you get defensive, try asking the people who love you. They know. They're totally on your side, but you get defensive with them, too. Everyone gets defensive. But you get to choose how you deal with the defensive feelings that push your buttons.

It would be great if there were a "listening angel" who followed us through our day. Every time a situation came up that threatened our sense of competency or well-being, the angel would whisper, "Fear not!" and reassure us that as God's beloved child, we can handle whatever anyone has to say to us or about us.

We could all use this help because listening threatens our self-esteem. We feel pressure from the people we lead to have answers that will fix their drug-addicted kids, heal their marriages, and make all their pain go away. We would like to be superhuman heroes for them, but we're not.

Most of us have tried and failed at "fixing" people. Here's another job for the listening angel. The voice we need to hear in this case says, "Fear not! You are not the Savior. It's not up to you to fix every broken thing. Let go of that idolatry, and give the most precious gift you possess—the undivided attention of your heart and mind." Another important whisper might go, "Fear not! This is not about you. God will increase as you decrease."

After spending over twenty years struggling to heal the hurting and fix the recalcitrant and stubborn people in his ministry, pastor Steve Sjogren calls himself a recovering answer-man. Steve says:

> *For a while, being a kind of cosmic Shell Answer Man may pump up your sense of self-importance, but it's a bad deal for everyone involved. It doesn't truly help people, and it sets you up for a serious ego-correcting fall. These days I'm learning that the more humbly I listen to people, the better I can hear God...*
>
> *I am laying aside my agenda and trying to listen from the heart. As I lay my life down and listen to the individual in front of me, I end up having far greater insight and a greater impact on each individual in much less time. God increases when I decrease.[9]*

There is great freedom in laying down our emotional need to be God's answer-man or answer-woman. Usually the most powerful help we can give people who are struggling with pain is *not* advice. Have you ever tried to figure out the right thing to say at a funeral? Many times doing the right thing in this difficult time means *not* saying anything at all. Instead of a word, offer a listening ear, a hand to squeeze, and the silent encouragement of your presence.

We may still be afraid of what others think or that they might believe we agree with them when we don't. Many of our students have expressed concern that if they practice these listening methods with non-Christians, these uncorrected sinners will think that they are endorsing their lifestyle choices. We need to let go of this fear. By practicing Christlike listening, we communicate love and understanding. Trying to understand people's actions or lifestyle choices is not the same as agreeing with them. By our listening, we are beginning a conversation that may open the door for sharing our perspective. On the other hand, dispensing correction without listening inevitably leads to alienation and fruitless, quick-to-anger confrontations.

> Trying to understand people's actions or lifestyle choices is not the same as agreeing with them.

Now take a few minutes to assess your own attitudes about listening by completing the exercise on page 144.

The bottom line is that losing control (or the illusion that we ever had it) is a very good thing. Breaking the barriers we've discussed in this chapter is a long-term process that requires becoming more aware of the functional and dysfunctional ways we operate as human beings and as leaders. In the next chapter, we'll focus on discovering and understanding our unique leadership temperaments and the blessings and barriers they bring with them.

▮▮▮ A Look in the Listening Mirror ▮▮▮

We've been told that most leaders spend about 70 percent of their waking hours (over eleven hours a day) participating in some form of verbal communication. The breakdown is as follows: We generally spend about 9 percent of our time writing, 16 percent reading, 35 percent talking, and (here's the big surprise) an average of 40 percent listening.[10] Use the "listening mirror" to gauge your attitudes and beliefs about time spent listening. Look at each column and decide whether your current attitudes are closer to the left or right.

L i s t e n i n g . . .

is not my job.	comes before all my other jobs.
slows things down.	ultimately speeds everything up.
looks weak and indecisive.	is a sign of openness and confidence.
isn't a productive use of my time.	is worth every second it takes.
opens the door to criticism.	opens the door to understanding.
stirs up uncomfortable emotions.	reveals what's really happening.
is for soft, effeminate leaders.	is for any leader who wants results.

1. List the listening barriers you need to work on breaking.

2. For each barrier you listed, what will you do to begin to change?

3. Name a person you want to listen to effectively while trying to eliminate these barriers.

ENDNOTES

1. C.S. Lewis, *Mere Christianity* (New York, NY: Macmillan Publishing Company, 1952), 6.

2. Brian J. Dodd, *Empowered Church Leadership: Ministry in the Spirit According to Paul* (Downers Grove, IL: InterVarsity Press, 2003), 154.

3. Ibid., 155.

4. Morgan W. McCall Jr., Michael M. Lombardo, and Ann M. Morrison, *The Lessons of Experience: How Successful Executives Develop on the Job* (Lexington, MA: Lexington Books, 1988).

5. Bob Briner and Ray Pritchard, *The Leadership Lessons of Jesus: A Timeless Model for Today's Leaders* (Nashville, TN: Broadman & Holman Publishers, 1997), 33.

6. John Ortberg, Laurie Pederson, and Judson Poling, *Groups: The Life-Giving Power of Community* (Grand Rapids, MI: Zondervan, 2000).

7. Laurie Beth Jones, *Jesus, CEO: Using Ancient Wisdom for Visionary Leadership* (New York, NY: Hyperion, 1995), 180-181.

8. Henri J. M. Nouwen, *Bread for the Journey: A Day Book of Wisdom and Faith* (San Francisco, CA: HarperCollins Publishers, 1996), March 11.

9. Steve Sjogren, Dave Ping, and Doug Pollock, *Irresistible Evangelism* (Loveland, CO: Group Publishing, Inc., 2004), 114.

10. Malcolm Webber, "Listening: Why Listening Is Important," Leadership Letters (Leadership Letter #58, August 15, 2003).

"So he came to a town in Samaria called Sychar, near the plot of ground Jacob had given to his son Joseph. Jacob's well was there, and Jesus, tired as he was from the journey, sat down by the well. It was about the sixth hour.

"When a Samaritan woman came to draw water, Jesus said to her, 'Will you give me a drink?'" (John 4:5-7).

9

Listening at JACOB'S WELL

You've heard this story at least a hundred times. You know exactly who the Jewish traveler was who came to Jacob's well that day. You know why the woman he'd spoken to left her water jar, ran back through town, and told everyone who'd so cruelly shunned her to come and listen to this amazing stranger.

But have you ever stopped to wonder what caused the townspeople to listen to and follow her? What suddenly transformed her from a social leper into someone who could inspire a whole town full of people to leave their jobs unfinished and their housework half done, to drop everything that was so important to them and follow her out into the noonday heat? They must have recognized that something truly amazing was going on. This joyful woman was no longer the ostracized outsider who'd quietly crept in and out of town all those years. She was unashamed. She was shouting and ecstatically pointing the way to the man who'd known all about her life and, in spite of everything she'd done, had offered her living water. The Messiah had come to their town, and she was his messenger!

Just as he had turned water into wine at Cana, in a matter of minutes, Jesus turned the least likely person in Sychar into the leader he would use to bring the whole town to himself. It's true, the people only followed her until they found Jesus and heard him themselves, but isn't that what a leader in Christ's kingdom is called to do? Aren't we to forget ourselves and constantly bring others to the source of hope, healing, and transformation? Isn't helping others find and follow Jesus what leadership is all about?

Yes, it was the woman's testimony that caused the townspeople to come to Jesus, but what they saw for themselves made them invite him into their homes and hearts. Imagine how the disciples must have been scandalized at the way Jesus interacted with this "fallen woman." He violated time-honored social customs that prohibited a rabbi from speaking directly even to respectable women. Then this woman usurped the disciples' job of announcing the Messiah—and she announced him in Samaria! Passing through this forsaken country had been an annoying inconvenience, a necessary but distasteful detour among an unclean and unworthy race of blasphemers. But Jesus didn't see it that way. He had another plan.

Jesus not only wanted to bring salvation to these Samaritans but also sought to reveal something incredibly liberating to all of his disciples. To those who were present with him that day in Sychar and those who read John's account even today, Jesus was proclaiming release from the bondage Scripture speaks of in Jeremiah 2:13: "My people have committed two sins: They have forsaken me, the spring of living water, and have dug their own cisterns, broken cisterns that cannot hold water."

Like the disciples, we all have images of ministry, leadership, and listening we've picked up from our culture and upbringing. Too often, we allow the prejudices and habits that our society reinforces to become the "broken cisterns" we use to try to capture and dispense Christ's living water. Ultimately, we realize these man-made ways of operating just won't hold water, but where can we turn to find Christ-like alternatives?

The last thing we want to do in this book is shake a finger of blame in anyone's direction. As Dave loves to say, "We're all Bozos on this bus." Most leaders already feel guilty and deficient enough. Some of the leadership books we've read and seminars we've attended add fuel to our sense of inadequacy by describing humanly unattainable leadership profiles. Though not every book or seminar agrees on all the particulars, the picture that typically emerges is of a sharp, single-minded CEO who knows the Bible backward and forward. She is an outstanding communicator. He's warm, caring, genuine, and diplomatic. She is assertive and decisive but also sensitive, gentle, and approachable. He is able to leap tall buildings with a single bound...You know the rest.

We need to get over some of our unrealistic and culturally unbalanced images of what leadership means. To find a more reasonable and biblical picture, perhaps a good place to start is to ask, "What does God need leaders for? What functions does God want us to fulfill?"

Go ahead and think about it. God may not actually *need* human leaders, but he chooses to use them anyway. What are some of the things he wants to accomplish through them? Use the space below to list at least five major functions you think God raises up leaders to fulfill.

As we answered this question for ourselves, at least four functions came to mind right away. They also appear on most of the lists people make as they answer these questions for themselves.

First, God is looking for leaders to do what the woman at the well did so well—to uncompromisingly *proclaim* Jesus by asking people in villages, towns, and cities around the world, "Could this be the Messiah you've been waiting for?"

Second, we want to *teach* those who respond to the good news how to get to know Jesus by reading and applying the Bible's wisdom to their daily lives.

Third, we need leaders to help us joyfully praise God, celebrate his love for us, and *worship* him.

Fourth, we want leaders who can help us *connect* with and find practical ways to love one another and to live as a family that supports every member's healing and growth.

Some have suggested that God is raising up an *army* to charge the gates of hell and set the captives free. He is organizing a *school* where every believer can learn the essential attitudes and skills needed for following and serving Jesus. He is throwing a *party* at which we can shed our self-consciousness and experience God's presence with praise and thanksgiving. God is also establishing a *family* in which each of us can find a safe place to belong and be held accountable to continually heal and grow in Christlikeness. (We'll talk more about growth and healing in Chapter 11.) In each of these models, God uses certain kinds of leaders!

Where Listening Comes In

Whether he needs them or not, God *chooses to use* imperfect humans to encourage, motivate, confront, and continually build up all of these functions within his body (Ephesians 4:12). Sometimes we do it in our own cracked and leaky ways that can't hold water (Jeremiah 2:13). Sometimes we are quick to listen to God and people and to let the living water do its work.

We believe that the overall success and health of each of these functions depends on leaders who practice Christlike listening. You simply can't share Christ effectively if you don't know how to listen. Many who try it only succeed in alienating countless souls that remain captive, separated from God. You can't teach and disciple without taking the time to understand the needs and desires of learners and followers. Even leading worship is an exercise in listening to God and tuning in to people's hearts. Yes, the music is important, but we've all experienced fine musicianship and great talent that didn't help us focus our hearts on worship. Finally, it probably should be obvious that families that don't listen well are what counselors call *dysfunctional*. This is especially true of God's family. All of the seven circles of disunity we discussed in Chapter 3 flow from poor listening.

The army, school, party, and family functions are all essential to the healthy growth and continuation of the body of Christ. Each function depends on the other three, and all four functions depend on relationships in which we both listen and speak truth in love. From the time the book of James was penned to the present day, healthy churches and believers have had to attend carefully to each of these life-giving functions and to the work of being quick to listen. No church or individual can stay healthy for very long if it neglects any of them.

Leadership Temperaments

As we've worked with leaders and churches around the world, we've noticed that most leaders are attracted to one or two of these four functions of the church. They love serving in the army much more than the school or facilitating the party more than nurturing family relationships. We are logically happiest serving in the areas we like and in which we are good. We may also have greater passion for those roles in which we've received the most blessing. However, it also seems that God specifically calls and gifts people into one or two of these areas. We each have our own "ministry temperament" that leads us to value our preferred niche over the others. Since the army, the school, the party, and the family each require a specific type of service, each function tends to produce a different kind of leadership temperament. Read the following descriptions, and think about how they relate to you and the leaders you know.

1. The Commander or Army-Style Leader

If you are drawn to the proclamational or *army* function of leading, you will probably cultivate leadership qualities that allow you to influence others and direct them toward specific goals. You may naturally think in terms of objectives and the strategies necessary to accomplish them.

As a Commander, you are probably a fairly competitive person who relishes playing hard and doing whatever it takes to win. You may be conscious of your drive to succeed at every task you undertake, or may never have given it a second thought because it's just part of who you are. You are a practical person who quickly grasps what needs to be done and then attacks it using all the gifts and resources at your disposal.

You have a positive passion for action and getting things done the right way the first time. You're a take-charge kind of person who sees just what needs to be done and how to go about doing it effectively. Like it or not, and with varying levels of tact, you frequently find your-self giving orders—or at least strongly suggesting what others should do or how they should think. You have a specific picture of the way you want things done and tend to get frustrated with anything that might get in the way of your plan.

Many will follow your lead with a sense of relief that someone is really in charge. Others will feel stifled, irritated, or bulldozed by your forceful style of getting things done. They may complain that you've ignored their input and left them out of the process. In your heart of hearts, you may have a difficult time not labeling these people as rebellious whiners or malcontents.

If you identify strongly with our description of the Commander, you are the person for whom many churches and organizations are longing. They're looking for someone like you to lead the charge *for them*. You are a strong visionary with a sense of purpose and urgency. You're a man or woman with a plan and the chutzpah to make it hap-pen. On the other hand, you're probably no diplomat, and when your strengths reign free, you have made (or are likely to make) enemies who will line up to fight you or work behind your back to undermine you. Other Commanders will tend to compete with you for control of people and resources, but you probably have a strategy for dealing with them as well.

If you don't immediately identify with the Commander, don't write it off yet. You may be like Dave's wife, Pam. Pam operates as a Commander in her private world and is very effective and efficient at ordering her work life. She has very strong opinions about what should be done, who should do it, and how it should be carried out. Pam's traditional upbringing, however, taught her that women should be modest and keep their ideas and opinions to themselves. Although she gladly offers help and advice to any who seek her out, instead of giving orders and forcefully communicating her ideas, she often keeps them inside her head where they frustrate her but don't bother anyone else.

Pam is a *frustrated* Commander. Her predisposition is to take charge and get the job done, but like many women, she avoids appear-ing too pushy or demanding. These assertive qualities are generally seen as highly desirable in men, but many women have been taught that they are unladylike. Pam has learned to avoid criticism by "leading from behind" or subtly feeding her ideas and instructions to Dave and others, thereby diverting the spotlight from herself.

Throughout their marriage, Dave has had to encourage Pam to speak up and share her wise insights and capacity for strategic thinking openly and directly. Like Pam, many women (and men) have lots of different reasons for hiding their leadership light "under a bushel," but when they do, everybody loses. The church loses valuable gifts of guidance they could provide, and they lose the joy of using their God-given abilities and the opportunity to hone and refine them.

Every Commander needs to temper his or her take-charge tendencies with quick-to-listen leadership. But quashing these tendencies altogether is unhealthy. People like Pam are champion mobilizers when given the opportunity. Suppressing the Commander spirit within them leads to depression and unhappiness. Church leaders who do this are like the hands telling the feet, "I don't need you." This is surely not pleasing to the Head of the body, who honored the dishonored woman at the well.

If only some parts of this description describe you, it's very possible that Commander is your secondary leadership preference. Either way, it's a style you shouldn't shy away from embracing. You may not have expected to hear this in a book about listening, but your temperament is invaluable to the body of Christ. As you acknowledge that this is how you're wired, you can maximize your leadership strengths by becoming a more proactive listener who strategically encourages others of differing leadership temperaments.

Even if you don't see yourself anywhere in the Commander description, you can probably pick out a few Commanders in your church or organization. Understanding them and discovering the similarities and differences between this style and your own leadership temperament can help you become more effective.

2. The Performer or Party-Style Leader

If you are drawn to the celebrational or *party* function of the body, you will cultivate qualities that help you create captivating experiences that inspire, entertain, or produce a strong emotional impact. If you deeply desire to present people with experiences that make Christ's message come alive in their hearts and minds, you may be a Performer.

As a Performer, you're probably drawn to drama, music, and storytelling that engage people and capture their attention. You thrive on thinking creatively and engaging people emotionally. You love connecting with other people's life experiences and then carefully and creatively offering them new perspectives. You may instinctively gravitate to analogies, metaphors, and a rich variety of stories and word pictures. You revel in using your imagination and all five senses to open new doors of experience for yourself and others. Experiencing God and helping others experience God's presence are passionate and constant quests for you. Performers express themselves by creating visual art, writing and performing music, speaking in public, or any of a wide variety of expressions that engage or entertain others.

If you're a Performer, your ability to tune in to the things that engage people gives you great influence, but it can also trap you into living for external approval. Your human hunger to be understood and treated as special can drive you to pull out all the stops as you seek to please and impress those around you. You feel most alive when you're performing, but this feeling can become subtly addicting as your emotions begin to feed on audience appreciation. Eventually, you may not know what to do without an audience to give you cues and let you know how you are doing.

Performer leaders don't have to be raving extroverts. To be a Performer, you don't have to be a star or a personality. Some Performers have all the tendencies mentioned above yet are painfully self-conscious and shy. Sir Laurence Olivier, one of the greatest stage performers of all time, reputedly suffered nervousness and self-consciousness that caused him to throw up before nearly every performance. Being deeply aware of how others may perceive you is actually an important quality in a Performer.

Many times, shy people are frustrated or damaged Performers who have learned to keep their inner artistry hidden for fear of being ridiculed. Sadly, we are often very cruel to anyone in the process of discovering and refining performing skills—even in the church. The passion for excellence that the business and show-business worlds have exported into many of our churches often leaves little room for learning or making mistakes. Only the very best need apply, and by the way, "Don't call us; we'll call you." This is an incredible loss to the church.

Interestingly, churches that allow only certain people to appear up front are usually led by highly successful Performers. In many ways, these churches have become theaters, filled with highly critical congregational audiences who won't stand for any show that isn't ready for prime time. Whether the audience is large or small, yielding the stage to others with different ideas, different gifts, and different levels of experience can be a real challenge for the Performer. Just as the Commander may have difficulty learning to share the field with other Commanders, Performers may find it tough to allow other Performers with varying levels of talent to share the stage.

Every church needs Performer leaders whose talents have been encouraged and allowed to develop. Their specific abilities inspire us, improve our morale, and make the experience of following the Lord far more exciting. Performers can make God's vision come alive in a way we can truly feel. With their help, we will be able to *taste and see* more of what God has in mind for us.

If you're a Performer, churches and mission groups are crying out for leaders like you who have even the undeveloped potential to captivate and inspire us. If you're shy, it may be hard to admit that this could be you and that you bring these great strengths to the table. But if this sounds even a little bit like you, by all means, step onto the stage! Becoming quick to listen will allow you to shine in your strengths and get help in the areas in which you need to work. By working together with the Commanders, Scholars, and Parents in your church or organization, you will find clear direction, accountability, and encouragement. As a Performer, you can probably easily imagine what that kind of community might be like.

3. The Scholar or School-Style Leader

If you are drawn to the *educational* or *school* function of the body, you will cultivate qualities that allow you to help people dig into the Bible and excavate its life-giving Truth. You're naturally attracted to researching, discovering, and explaining knowledge that allows believers to become more obedient disciples. You think and reason deeply, and your thoughts lead to deliberations, questions, and profound conclusions. You probably enjoy the mental exercise of a good debate, not because you enjoy arguing for its own sake but because you relish the insight that comes in the process.

As a Scholar, you enjoy collecting as much information, research, theological insight, and confirmatory evidence as you can to back up your conclusions. You're probably very good at studying sociological or organizational trends and interpreting what they may imply about future choices. You work diligently to inform your followers by organizing what you've learned through your own in-depth study. You automatically evaluate and critique everything you hear, read, or see on any given topic, storing pertinent information away for future reference. When your ideas are challenged, you like to be ready with the most recent data to support your point of view.

People turn to Scholars when they are making important decisions that put a great deal of time or money at stake. They respect your intellect, hard-won wisdom, and studied insight and appreciate your ability to analyze risks and ask the really tough questions. Since you revel in the world of ideas, you also enjoy challenging yourself and others to see new possibilities latent in the situations around you.

Scholars are often skeptical of the emotional appeals of the Performer and Parental temperaments, preferring cold, hard facts to passionate convictions. You are partial to careful research that weighs all available data rather than excited experiential claims and testimonies. Although Performer and Parental leaders may see your scholarly tendencies as a wet blanket cast over their enthusiasm, every church and organization desperately needs scholarly leaders. Scholars provide the depth of insight and critical perspective that slows us down. Scholars help us stop and think before charging recklessly into seemingly attractive but potentially disastrous decisions.

There was a time being an insightful Scholar was *the* prime qualification for leadership in a church. Studying and clearly explaining the Word of God was valued above all other leadership qualities. Today, however, scholarship generally takes a back seat, and Scholars are often discounted or relegated to institutions of higher learning. Leaders and potential leaders with a scholarly bent who are not credentialed professors at nearby colleges often find their input unwelcome in today's fast-paced churches.

If you identify with some of what we've written about Scholar leaders, you probably find it increasingly difficult to contribute and lead in today's churches. Modesty may also make it difficult to acknowledge your invaluable role in keeping our churches on course and helping us steer clear of the hidden disasters we'll inevitably encounter along the way. Though you may feel like a lone voice crying in the wilderness, rest assured that your voice is desperately needed—now more than ever. Although people may be less impressed with scholarly leadership than in the past and less inclined to hang on your every word, we need Scholars to step forward and bring balance to the other three essential leadership temperaments.

4. The Parent or Family-Style Leader

Last but certainly not least, if you are drawn to the *relational* or *family* function of the body, you will cultivate qualities that allow you to nurture people and give them a safe atmosphere to genuinely be themselves. You're good at serving, encouraging, and supporting people through the various awkward stages that come with spiritual babyhood, childhood, adolescence, and even maturity.

As a Parent leader, you just can't resist caring for needy people who require lots of help and encouragement. Your heart almost involuntarily goes out to broken and immature people who need a helping hand to become healthier, better-adjusted followers of Jesus. You love people as a parent would love them, and you express your love by nurturing, serving, and protecting. You accept people where they are, but you're not content until you've encouraged and empowered them to become the people you know God intends for them to be. You put a high priority on being available and mentoring people for growth. Meeting people's needs is your passion!

Nurturing others is something you almost do without thinking—it's just part of who you are. You build strong, compassionate, loyal relationships and then fiercely protect them. You remember important dates and celebrate important milestones in others' lives with gifts or kind words that show them that you're on their team. Sometimes you may care so much that it's a challenge not to overprotect or smother people with your concern. Like many parents, you may also find it very difficult to let go and allow others to grow up and take full responsibility for themselves.

Being a Parent leader can be a mixed blessing for you and for those you care about. You are bound to disappoint and be disappointed by the people you reach out to help. Like natural parenting, this kind of leadership is fraught with intense emotional highs and devastating lows.

Though a growing number of books and sermons trumpet the value of caring relationships, many Commanders, Performers, and Scholars may still look down on relational Parent leaders, accusing them of being too emotional or touchy-feely. Although our streets and churches are filled with people desperately looking for what Parent leaders have to offer, many potentially outstanding relational leaders hide their lights for fear of being labeled and discounted by insensitive leaders whose idea of relationship is restricted to superficial conversations between rounds of golf.

Some Parent leaders hesitate to step forward because they fear the unhealthy dependence so many needy people bring to their search for a parent figure. If you think you may be a Parent leader, you've probably experienced this life-consuming drain on your energy and family time. You've felt torn between being an on-call Mr. or Ms. Fix-It for needy and frequently ungrateful people and having time for a healthy life and family of your own. Becoming a quick-to-listen leader will help you learn to come alongside others without assuming responsibility for their lives. Once you're free of this unhealthy load, you'll probably find relational leadership safe and enjoyable again.

Each of the four basic leadership temperaments (Commander, Performer, Scholar, Parent) carries with it powerfully positive and significantly challenging characteristics. Each leadership temperament meets an essential need in the body of Christ and for the individual leaders within it. However, without the other three temperaments, each type of leader is grossly inadequate. We need one another keenly and are doomed to fail if even one temperament is missing. Every spiritually vital congregation needs a dynamic balance of all four leadership temperaments.

The four leadership temperaments are like the medical vital signs doctors and health care professionals use to quickly evaluate the state of our physical bodies. A nurse checks our temperature, respiration, pulse, and blood pressure. If any *one* of these indicators is outside of a relatively narrow healthy range, the doctor knows we are sick.

In the same way, we know the body of Christ is in trouble when the vital outreach, worship, discipleship, or relational functions of the church lack an ongoing supply of leaders. When any area is neglected or allowed to dominate the others, the church will sicken and eventually die spiritually. The body of Christ can't stay healthy by specializing in one or two areas and ignoring the others any more than our physical bodies can stay alive without breathing, pumping blood, or regulating our body temperature. Outside of Jesus himself, no one leader could ever be adequate. And even Jesus depends on the Father and the Holy Spirit.

Primary Leadership Temperaments

As we've said, every person reading this book will naturally favor one of these four temperaments of leadership as a primary style. If you're having a hard time deciding your primary approach, look at the chart on page 160. Use the scale at the bottom of the chart to determine which temperament is closest to your own. On a scale of one to five, with one being least like you and five being most like you, where do you see yourself?

As you review the chart, notice that each orientation has a preferred way of leading. The Commander will probably find himself or herself wanting to *tell* people what to do. Commanders can usually sketch out a concrete picture of a desired outcome and provide at least a basic plan for how to reach that destination. The Commander temperament is excellent for *mobilizing* people and getting those who are already motivated to move in the same direction in a coordinated way. The Commander's objective is always in view, and his or her goal is to win no matter what the odds.

The Performer leads by *showing* the way and providing exciting experiences that *motivate* people to join him or her. Performers offer fresh tastes of what might be ahead for people who are willing to join them on the journey. Performers seek to make an emotional impact on people's lives that will move them forward toward God.

Scholars lead by *questioning* and challenging people to think. Scholars encourage people to examine the facts for themselves and help *correct* any false assumptions that might arise in the process. The Scholar's goal is to *persuade* people to follow the path of obedient discipleship.

Parents lead by demonstrating *caring* and encouraging people toward personal healing and growth. The Parent leader's goal is to *nurture* and support people to develop the life in Christ they've always wanted.

No matter what your leadership temperament might be, two things are true about you. First, your gifts, talents, and leadership temperament are desperately needed to "prepare God's people for works of service" (Ephesians 4:12). Other gifts are also needed, but that doesn't mean yours aren't a critically important ingredient. Second, none of us, and none of our individual leadership temperaments, is sufficient for the task. We need God, and we need each other.

Listening can be the critical link that allows us to function and cooperate together as a body. Ephesians 4:15-16 says, "Instead, speaking the truth in love, we will in all things grow up into him who is the Head, that is, Christ. From him the whole body, joined and held together by every supporting ligament, grows and builds itself up in love, as each part does its work." Did you catch that first phrase? So simple, yet so critical: Speaking the truth in love.

At the beginning of this chapter, we talked about one woman's actions that enabled a whole town to hear Christ's words. She isn't one who is usually singled out as a role model. Yes, she had a sinful past. But she hadn't systematically persecuted Christians or been an accessory to murder as the Apostle Paul had. She hadn't shamefully denied Jesus three times as Peter had. She was as unworthy as all of us are. The good news is that the same Jesus who knew everything she'd ever done also knows all about us. And even though he knows us, he still wants us to lead in his name. He wants his living water to spring up within us so he can bring eternal life to *our* villages and churches and families. We can do it—if we listen and work together.

Commander	Performer	Scholar	Parent
LEADS BY **telling**	LEADS BY **showing**	LEADS BY **questioning**	LEADS BY **caring**
• takes charge • dictates strategy • delegates tasks	• presents experiences • demon- strates talents • offers possibilities	• researches data • studies trends • deliberates and debates	• meets needs • models behavior • protects and serves
GREAT AT **mobilizing**	GREAT AT **correcting**	GREAT AT **inspiring**	GREAT AT **encouraging**
• grasps vision • thinks strategically • engages action	• casts vision • thinks creatively • engages emotions	• evaluates vision • thinks thoroughly • engages intellect	• fleshes out vision • thinks relationally • engages people
END GOAL **to win**	END GOAL **to impact**	END GOAL **to persuade**	END GOAL **to nurture**
MY RATING: 1 2 3 4 5	MY RATING: 1 2 3 4 5	MY RATING: 1 2 3 4 5	MY RATING: 1 2 3 4 5

10

Listening
STYLES

W e've described the four basic leadership temperaments and how they affect the people around us. Since this is a book about listening, it's important to recognize that each temperament also has its own specific style of listening. Before we go any further, we should point out that no temperament has a lock on the skill of listening, but some temperaments will find it easier than others. That being said, if leaders of all temperaments practice in their areas of weakness and make the most of their ministry gifts, the listening differences between each temperament may be negligible. As you read this chapter, you may want to skip right to your own listening temperament, but resist the temptation. Getting a handle on how others operate may be as helpful or even more helpful than understanding your own approach.

Commander: Hyperfocus on Vision

As we've said, the Commander is frequently a highly sought-after leadership temperament. Unfortunately, Commanders also have the most difficulty listening to and valuing input from others—unless the input has a clear and direct bearing on the vision that drives this particular Commander. Vision and the specific objectives and tasks needed to bring it about stand at the very epicenter of the Commander's motivations. Purpose and vision are not just the main event; they are practically the *only* event.

Leaders of other temperaments may view this hyperfocus as insensitive or unkind, but the Commander evaluates every task and relationship according to whether it serves or detracts from the central cause. Like their military namesakes, Commanders prefer to give orders and tell people what to do without wasting time in the process. When the Commander talks, others are expected to listen. This is not to say Commanders don't care how others feel or what they think. They're just utterly convinced that personal feelings and agendas (even their own) pale in comparison to the urgent task of fulfilling the larger mission.

If you're a Commander, you're tenacious in pursuing anything that will help accomplish your essential objectives. When you read a book, you quickly skim through, highlighter in hand, looking for practical points that will help you get where you're going or convince others of the rightness of your cause. The loyal people around you can feel your passion, but what they often hunger for is your *compassion.* Commander: You may value, trust, and even love your followers, but they won't know it unless you take the time to show it—and that means listening.

Our ministry was called in to consult with a powerhouse church that had been growing at an incredible rate. It had a truly spectacular vision and a powerful Commander leader at the helm. It also had a spectacular staff turnover rate. The church had lost five key staff people in as many months. We were fortunate enough to get the leaders of this church to take time out of their busy schedules to sit down and listen to one another.

After some tentative discussion between the head pastor and the rest of his staff, it was clear we weren't getting anywhere. So we asked the leader to listen to his staff for a while—without interrupting to explain or defend his big-picture vision. We also asked the staff members to think of some word pictures that might communicate how it felt for them to be working in that church. A very sharp, young, female staff member hesitantly gave us all a picture we will never forget:

> *Working here is like driving a high performance race car in the Indianapolis 500. The best cars and racing professionals have come from all over the country to be here. Expectations are high, and the pressure to win is astronomical. We get out on the track, and we give it all we have, lap after lap after lap. When the time comes to pull into the pit to refuel and get new tires, the pit is empty. There is no pit crew, no gasoline, and no new tires. Then someone shouts at you to get back out there and win the race!*
>
> *It's about time someone asked why so many of us are crashing and burning and why so many are running out of gas before the race is over.*

What a wake-up call! This young lady's story captured the essence of what had been missing in that church. To the Commander's credit, he got the message loud and clear. Instead of trying to defend himself or his previous policies, he confessed and repented on the spot. It wasn't just the emotion of the moment either. He saw what a huge strategic mistake he'd been making with his leaders. He realized that the fuel his team needed to succeed was simple listening. The tires his extraordinary racers needed to run on were the one-on-one moments when they felt heard and valued.

If you're a Commander who wonders, "How will being quick to listen and slow to speak help me accomplish the vision God has entrusted to me?" read carefully. *All people are not like you.* They, too, serve the vision but in different ways, for different reasons. They may appreciate your occasional public acknowledgment, but they need more fuel to keep running. They need to know that they are personally important and even loved by their leader. When people believe that you care about their needs, that you are taking the time to understand them, and that you value them above what they can do for you, they won't just follow; they will lead others to the vision. They will also follow your example as they raise up and care for their own followers.

Commander leaders need to understand that listening is strategic.

It's not for the weak or faint of heart. It's not for anyone who places his or her own ego needs above those of others. Like most things of high value, it also has a high cost. Listening is not just an optional tool to add to your leadership toolbox; it's a fundamental calling for every servant leader. If you really want to follow your vision forward to be the church God intended, you must begin to truly listen. The Commander pastor we described earlier took listening training for himself and was so convinced of its benefit that he now requires it of anyone in his church who aspires to lead.

Quick-to-Listen Commanders

You've heard the old saying "the devil is in the details." When it comes to building and maintaining vision, it's often the little stuff that we do or don't do that makes the greatest difference. Listening is one of those very powerful little things.

If you are a Commander leader, you'll be tempted to think in terms of grand strategies, innovative organizational structures, and bold new approaches that will help you change some part of the world in exciting ways. A few years ago, we heard Wayne Cordeiro, a pastor of New Hope Christian fellowship in Honolulu, Hawaii, explain a profound principle he'd discovered in the process of growing his church and consulting with visionary leaders of similarly dynamic congregations.[1] During its first six years, Wayne's church has seen more than 7,800 people become Christians for the first time. The church has now grown to over 9,000 weekend attendees. To facilitate this growth, Wayne studied several popular organizational structures and ministry models and determined that *all of them work* as long as they are built on genuinely healthy relationships. Conversely, *none* of the models he studied or tried work for long in the absence of healthy relationships. *Listening is the cement of healthy relationships.*

> The quality and cohesion of the cement that holds up our churches, mission organizations, or Christian businesses are determined by how well we hear one another and speak the truth in love.

No matter how well a building is designed, if the cement that holds everything together is defective, the building will crumble. The quality and cohesion of the cement that holds up our churches, mission organizations, or Christian businesses are determined by how well we hear one another and speak the truth in love. As we've said, many Commanders are notoriously quick to speak without taking adequate time to strengthen their understanding and connection with key leaders and followers around them.

As a Commander, you may indeed speak truth from first-class motivations. But before your followers can receive it, they need to see that you care about and respect them. At this point, you may hear a cranky voice within you complaining, "Can't they see how hard I work? Isn't it enough that I provide them with vision and every little thing they need to carry it out? Can't they figure it out for themselves?" Sorry, but no, they can't. Remember, they may not be like you. They want and deserve some quality time focused on your relationship with them. Like Jesus, you can choose to give more to the three closest to you than to the twelve, and more to the twelve than the seventy, and so on, but your people need to have your ear. This is where proactive listening comes in.

Don't wait around until people are feeling weary and unappreciated. Follow the Father's example and run out to meet them. Start with one person. Pursue that person and say, "If you have a few minutes, I'd like to hear how things are going with you."

As a Commander, you'll be tempted to focus the conversation on the tasks and objectives that are on your mind, but don't. Find out how *the other person* feels and what's happening with his or her family. If you have time, request feedback about how the person's ministry job is going. This follower may be hesitant at first but, when he or she senses that you don't have any hidden agendas, will begin to respond to your attention like a wilting flower does to water and light.

Although it may chafe at your Commander nature, assign a high priority to these "listening appointments." Remember, having a proactive ear to the ground will help you understand and prepare for any relational storms that might be brewing among the troops. Armed with this understanding, you'll no longer find yourself having to second-guess people's thoughts and feelings when things go awry. The higher the value you place on creating and maintaining relational connections, the more you will gain from what's to come. Maintaining these connections will also help you understand the leadership and listening approaches of others.

Performer: Hyperfocus on "Vibe"

Performer leaders naturally value listening. This doesn't automatically mean they are good at it, but their innate leadership temperament drives them to be more outwardly oriented. Performers tune in to the subtle, nonverbal cues that tell them how people are responding. Without thinking much about it, Performers are constantly adjusting what musicians and stage performers call "the vibe."

As a Performer, your emotional feelers are always taking the temperature of whatever's happening around you. You subconsciously shape most, if not all, of what you do in reference to how others might experience it. You delight in making people laugh, feel, or think deeply. You are also often painfully conscious of how others react or fail to react to these efforts.

To Performers, impressions and appearances are critically important, not for their own sake but because they reflect the Performer's success or failure as a leader. If people seem happy, excited, and upbeat, the Performer will usually feel the same way. Performers live for this kind of energy and will often repeat behaviors that produce emotionally invigorating results.

Feeling on top of things and in control is very important to the Performer. You probably expend a great deal of energy keeping your followers in a positive state of mind. For this reason, actually pursuing listening may be difficult for you. Whenever you sense the vibe going sour, your tendency is to do whatever it takes to lighten things up. You may attempt to use humor, storytelling, or your own unique song and dance to buoy the spirits of followers. Sometimes this can be helpful; however, in many instances these followers are just looking for a little empathy. They don't want to be cheered up; they need to be heard.

> They don't want to be cheered up; they need to be heard.

The Performer's instinctive reaction to unpleasant or confused feelings is to attempt to shape them and move people in a more agreeable direction. The more anxious people get, the more you want to act in ways that soothe. The sadder they get, the more you need to lift their spirits. You have a lot of hero in you: rescuing damsels in distress, slaying boogeymen, and such. But the most authentically heroic thing you can do for your followers is not to rescue *them* from *their* feelings when *you* begin to feel uncomfortable. In this case, your wonderful sensitivity to feelings can actually work against you.

Avoiding the inevitable pain that comes with growth and healing is the Achilles heel that trips up many Performer leaders. You may recognize the value of facing troubles head on, but your hidden instinct tells you to use your talents to divert attention from them. Sometimes this process can be so subtle that you may not even know you are doing it. When pain, grief, or even mild unpleasantness begins to rear its head, you instinctively want to strike up the music and take the stage, just as Mickey Rooney and Judy Garland did in many of their 1940s movies. In those early movies, the solution to just about every problem began with "I know, Judy, let's put on a show!" Like Mickey and Judy, you can pull together entertaining musical and comedy numbers in a flash—no rehearsal required.

> The more amazing and impressive your performance is today, the more people will leave all the spiritual and intellectual heavy lifting up to you tomorrow.

Performer leaders frequently find it difficult to resist stepping into the spotlight to get the vision moving in the right direction. However, the job of listening to others requires you to keep the spotlight of your attention squarely on someone else's story. Their feelings, their thoughts, and their solutions take center stage. The other person is the star of this drama, and if there is a hero, it's not you. It's the Lord.

In this production, your role is backstage. Your job is to run the lights and draw the curtains at the right times so people can hear and see themselves in new ways. If you listen well, no one will notice you. Although it may be painful, you must allow the tension and the struggle to take place without diverting or interrupting it. This is one of the best ways to help people experience God's grace and truth for themselves. That's your real passion, after all. It's why you signed up to lead in the first place.

Creating unhealthy dependency is a powerful temptation to many Performer leaders. Since you thrive on affirmation and applause, it's easy to be lured into playing the role of all-knowing guru to fans who would rather be spoon-fed answers than take responsibility for their own problems. When you take the lead for others, they don't have to face their responsibilities or deal with any consequences. Instead of discovering solutions that could help them grow stronger and more confident, your followers become increasingly needy and dependent. Of course, this is a recipe for permanent immaturity for them and perpetual burnout for you.

If you find your presence increasingly indispensable at every decision-making meeting, you may have already become too competent for your own good. This sounds odd, but whenever you over-function or over-perform, others will generally under-perform. The law of diminishing returns kicks in, and the more amazing and impressive your performance is today, the more people will leave all the spiritual and intellectual heavy lifting up to you tomorrow.

When you are quicker to listen and slower to speak, others around you begin to think and act for themselves. Instead of looking to you for every little thing, they get to work and struggle and ultimately shine with a competence all their own. Your instinctive *feel* for doing and saying things that get results can make it very hard to allow them to do it their way, but in our experience, it's more than worth it in the end.

I (Dave) have trained many great teachers over the years, but I still struggle with keeping the spotlight on others at the appropriate times.

> *Several people have told me that I am a great person to have in the audience when they are teaching or preaching because I laugh out loud at all their jokes and they can tell by my facial expressions that I'm tracking with every word they say. One friend even offered to pay me to travel with him as his own personal Ed McMahon to his Johnny Carson.*

> *Although I love hearing them teach, these folks don't know that as I listen, there is a Performer voice inside me that is constantly saying, "No! Don't say it that way!" or "There is a much cooler illustration you could use right here!" or "Pause now and give that thought time to sink in." It doesn't matter who is up front or how good he or she is; part of me is vicariously on stage with him or her.*

> *It's not that I don't love and enjoy what they're saying. It's just that they never say it quite the way I would. Usually, the teacher I'm listening to is far smarter and more articulate than I am, but I still have to bite my tongue and work to listen and not to interrupt. I believe in listening with my whole heart, but I battle hard with the part of me that wants to hog the spotlight. When I succeed at listening, I know it's because God has blessed me with self-control and used it to build up his body.*

Quick-to-Listen Performers

The spiritual fruit of patience and self-control that listening demands doesn't grow naturally the way weeds do. It requires special attention and painstaking care. If you are a Performer, you probably know this better than leaders with any other temperament. Your challenge is to remember that, as a leader, *your fruit grows primarily on other people's trees.* It really doesn't matter how gifted you are or how well you perform—if your followers don't grow up to meet their potential, they are just an audience.

Your abilities as a Performer can be a two-edged sword. People love to watch as you do what you do. But sometimes *all they do* is watch. They may be lazy or intimidated by your talent. Either way, by balancing your innate gifts with other-focused listening, you can put the task of growth more squarely on your followers' shoulders.

Performers have a great listening advantage among leaders. Because they can intuitively sense what others are feeling, the mechanics of listening come much more easily. With the help of the listening skills in this book, you'll be able to focus on doing less and listening more. As you truly listen, the people around you will gratefully accept greater personal responsibility and eventually begin to use their own gifts and talents to lead others.

Scholar: Hyperfocus on Knowledge

Scholar leaders love the power and beauty of ideas and the words that convey them. As a Scholar, your search for compelling ideas inspires you to dig deep into the Word and a wide assortment of books, articles, and Web pages to ferret out the best and most intriguing verbal gems. Whether or not you have advanced degrees and impressive letters after your name, the people around you have come to respect and rely on your keen wisdom and astute insight. Since you are constantly seeking out and evaluating new information, your approach to listening is very different from the listening styles we've talked about so far.

Scholars are hunter-gatherers of interesting concepts and persuasive arguments. When Scholars listen, they take what they hear and begin to compare it to the other ideas they've gathered. If what they hear is unique, powerful, or interesting, they may store it away and catalog it for future reference. As a Scholar, if you hear something that bolsters an important argument or adds to your understanding of some truth you are seeking to unlock, it goes right into your files. Otherwise, you are likely to pass by without giving what you hear much notice.

Listening is learning to the Scholar. If you believe there is something to learn when a person is speaking, you give your full attention. If you hear something you've heard before or disagree with, you'll probably ignore or argue with the person. Since you are constantly adding to and correcting your own understanding, it's only natural to do this. When you correct someone's false or misleading assumptions, you're not doing it to show off; in your mind, you're doing the person a favor that you would appreciate yourself.

As a Scholar, you're just as caring and passionate as leaders of other temperaments—if not more so. However, your passions tend to focus on the world of ideas. Your loves, likes, dislikes, and hatreds mingle with your highly developed conceptions of right and wrong, truth, and justice. You may find yourself fighting for abstract principles that are very meaningful to you but nearly incomprehensible to others. Dave experienced this tendency growing up on a college campus where his mother and stepfather were professors of English literature and history.

> One Christmas, my folks invited some of their colleagues from their university departments over for a festive holiday meal. In the midst of small talk and friendly socializing over roast turkey and cranberry sauce, an intense debate broke out between two highly esteemed academicians from the English department. This debate rapidly escalated into a very unpleasant and un-holidaylike scene that resulted in one of the professors calling for his coat and leaving the party in an angry huff.
>
> I was very confused, so I asked my stepfather what had triggered the dispute. He smiled and said, "Dr. So-and-So was very upset because some of the others at the party wouldn't agree that Robert Burns was the greatest poet who ever lived."

Of course, this is an extreme case, but it highlights the difficulty non-scholars may have as they try to understand the intense conviction you feel around some of your most cherished ideas. Though other leaders and followers may respect your intense passion for ideas, often they don't feel genuinely respected by you. Your followers want you to know that they aren't simply debate partners. Instead of just loving their ideas, they want you to love, understand, and value them as people.

Because of your passion for knowledge and ideas, people tend to see you in a perpetual teacher or researcher role. When you analytically weigh and (verbally or nonverbally) dismiss their ideas, others can feel as if they're students being graded or, worse yet, subjects you're experimenting on. People may interpret your scholarly detachment and your habit of using the people around you to help you discover, explain, or debate truth as indications of an aloof and superior attitude.

Scholar leaders often quickly pass judgment after internally weighing diverse factors and information. Although Scholars may be engaged in a mental struggle to decide what's best, most ethical, or least disruptive to the overall goal, that's not what others see. Others only see Scholars calculating, arguing for conclusions, and blasting away at people's ideas. As a Scholar leader, you may not think your ideas are always better than everyone else's (and we hope you don't), but followers can easily jump to this conclusion about you. Non-scholars have a much harder time separating their ideas from their personhood. So when you reject a person's ideas without taking ample time to communicate understanding, that person feels personally unappreciated and discounted.

Quick-to-Listen Scholars

If you have a Scholar's temperament, you will find that being quick to listen can help you build stronger relational bridges than ever before. The temptation for you will be to confuse knowing *about* listening and speaking the truth in love with *doing* it. You may be able to recite all the reasons for becoming a more Christlike and effective listener, but in this case, being right and knowledgeable will not help you become a better leader or, for that matter, a better friend. Becoming a quick-to-listen leader will require you to step out and put some of the ideas you've learned into action. As 2 Peter 1:6-7 admonishes, "to knowledge [add] self-control; and to self-control, perseverance; and to perseverance, godliness; and to godliness, brotherly kindness; and to brotherly kindness, love." All these ingredients are essential companions as you journey from good ideas to better, more respectful relationships.

Knowledge is temporary, but according to 1 Corinthians 13:8, "love never fails." Real love means knowing someone more fully and being more fully known. We may never experience the ultimate expression of this conjunction between love and knowledge until we stand before the Lord in heaven, but deep connections are available now if we truly listen and practice the good relational skills we do know. For Scholars, this is scary because it means stepping out of their role as an evaluator of ideas and stepping into more direct face-to-face human connections.

Not sure where to begin? Start with a same-sex friend whom you consider an intellectual peer. Set some appointments, and intentionally work to get to know the friend on a more personal level. Practice the Christlike active listening skills we talked about in Chapters 5 and 6. At first, try to listen at least five times more than you talk. Tune in to that person's feelings more than his or her thoughts, and try to keep your focus on demonstrating genuine concern. You will be amazed at how differently your friend responds to the kindness of listening. Once you have mastered these skills with peers, invite those you lead to share more of their feelings, concerns, and interests. As you learn to control your natural urge to evaluate and debate every idea, you will experience a whole new level of openness and cooperation in your ministry.

Parent: Hyperfocus on Emotions

Parent leaders are blessed with a sincere compassion for the feelings of others. Like Performers, their feelers always seek to pick up on others' moods and needs. If you're a Parent leader, your followers probably seek you out because they sense that you genuinely care. You're a safe port for them when they're stressed, confused, or angry. You're a shoulder to cry on and a ready source of encouragement.

Followers turn to Parent leaders anytime they need empathy and warmth and especially when they are in the midst of emotional turmoil or significant life-change. They're looking for a warmhearted and willing substitute for absent or disengaged biological parents, and they think you fit the bill. As a Parent leader, your heart resonates with Jesus' desire to gather his children "as a hen gathers her chicks under her wings" (Matthew 23:37). You are a gatherer who knows how to create a safe emotional nest where needy people can come for warmth and protection.

Parent leaders truly have a shepherd's heart. Following the example of the good shepherd in John 10:11, Parent leaders find practical ways to lay down their lives for the sheep. If you're a Parent leader, the wolves at your door had better beware because you are a passionate protector of those you shepherd. When you are aware of a need, you will sacrifice and do what you can to meet it. Whenever you hear a sheep bleating, you want to rush to the rescue!

While we all need loving parent figures to support us and help us make it over the bumps and potholes of life, there comes a time we must grow up and accept responsibility for ourselves. Some Parent leaders have a hard time embracing this truth. They don't listen and let go when they need to. Instead, they become compulsive protectors who over-nurture and over-control the people around them "for their own good."

At first, people love to be nurtured and protected. But as Parent leaders continue to overprotect and over-function, the people they are trying to lead become overdependant and under-responsible. When Parent leaders help people avoid the pain of growth, they condemn themselves to constant overwork. They will be eternally overwhelmed as they seek to meet ever-growing needs and put bandages on never-shrinking problems.

If you're a Parent leader, you may have a hard time listening because you know what you'll hear will be very painful. You may feel compelled to make the pain go away—the follower's pain *and your own*—by compulsively offering to do things for others that they are able but unwilling to do for themselves. If you recognize your listening weaknesses in this description, you're not alone. Although Parent leaders are among the most susceptible to this temptation, other leaders (and followers) have also succumbed. Churches and Christian organizations are filled with this kind of unhealthy, codependent enabling because very often we major in pain reduction and minor in speaking the truth in love.

Because of their deep sensitivity to others' feelings, Parent leaders may naturally avoid confrontation and giving honest, immediate feedback when it is needed. There is nothing more positively guaranteed to produce unhealthy, dysfunctional followers than a leader who backs off from speaking the truth in love. Though it may hurt for a moment, the health that comes from speaking the truth in love is almost always worth the risk of possible rejection. The cost of silence and unconfronted, lingering problems has ruined far more relationships and split many more congregations than speaking up in love ever could.

Quick-to-Listen Parents

As they seek to become quick to listen, Parent leaders need to practice respect and speaking the truth in love. Parent leaders who genuinely care about what's best for their followers will allow them to take on as much responsibility as they are able. To do anything less would be disrespectful of their God-given gifts and abilities. As leaders, we can't afford even the temporary good feeling that comes from being a papa bear or a mama bear at someone else's expense. Respect means leaving choices in the hands of the people they belong to instead of taking them away. If we want to do someone a favor, it's usually respectful to ask.

> The same irresponsible people who try to hand off their problems almost universally resent the people who take them on. They instinctively long for the dignity and respect that come with being treated in accordance with their true abilities.

People who make and face the real consequences of their own choices tend to act more responsibly and behave more intelligently than those we take care of. Sadly, our churches are filled with people who are more than willing to have us shoulder their responsibilities. Strangely enough, the same irresponsible people who try to hand off their problems almost universally resent the people who take them on. They instinctively long for the dignity and respect that come with being treated in accordance with their true abilities. This calls for great discernment, especially if you are a Parent leader who is prone to what we call "need-aholism."

Need-aholism is a lot like alcoholism. Instead of being unusually susceptible to overindulging in drink, "need-aholics" are prone to overindulge people who have an obvious need for help. Like an alcoholic craves liquor, they desperately crave the feeling that comes with being needed. If you are wondering if you might be a need-aholic, ask yourself,

▌ "Do I find it nearly impossible to say 'no' or to set healthy boundaries around time that I've set aside for my family or myself?"

▌ "Do I typically worry more about other people's problems than they do?"

▌ "Am I surrounded by people who couldn't function without my help?"

If you answered, "Yes, that sure sounds like me" to any of these questions, you are a prime candidate for Need-aholics Anonymous. If you said "no," it's possible that you're in denial; so ask your friends, spouse, or kids what they think. You may be surprised at their answers. If the truth still isn't clear, ask yourself this final question:

▌ "Do the people I care for look to me instead of God for help and 'salvation' from their pain?"

As Parent leaders, our primary task is to guide people into relationship with their God and Father!

Quick-to-Listen = Heart-to-Heart

The bottom line for all temperaments and listening styles is the same. Inherent in all of our natural approaches to leadership and listening are valuable leadership qualities as well as the seeds of serious problems. No matter what our temperaments are, we all occasionally succumb to the temptation to prize leaders of our own style above all others. But listening is the great leveler. Christ-centered listening compels the Commander to come down from her high horse, the Performer to step off the stage, the Scholar to descend from his lofty tower, and the Parent to step down from the place of authority. Christ-centered listening helps us recognize our need for one another and our need for God.

> Listening is the great leveler. Christ-centered listening compels the Commander to come down from her high horse, the Performer to step off the stage, the Scholar to descend from his lofty tower, and the Parent to step down from the place of authority.

In the final chapters, we'll focus on how you can use the skills and habits presented in this book to listen to what God has in mind for you and for the congregation, organization, ministry, or group that you lead.

ENDNOTE

1. Wayne Cordeiro, *Doing Church as a Team* (Honolulu, HI: New Hope Publishers, 1998). Wayne has written several other good books on leadership, including *Gems Along the Way, Attitudes That Attract Success, Living Life Above the Rubble, Indispensable Life Lessons,* and *Dream Releasers.*

" 'I will be a Father to you, and you will be my sons and daughters, says the Lord Almighty.' Since we have these promises, dear friends, let us purify ourselves from everything that contaminates body and spirit, perfecting holiness out of reverence for God" (2 Corinthians 6:18–7:1).

11

Listening for a Change: SPIRITUAL VITAL SIGNS

You've learned that every leader has a personal leadership temperament and listening style. You've identified your primary style as Commander, Performer, Scholar, or Parent. But how does knowing this information impact the specific church organization or group you lead? Should it change the kinds of leaders you are looking for? Should it change the way you equip them to lead? And where does being quick to listen and slow to speak fit in?

In this chapter we will try to answer these questions and talk about how to listen in some special ways that can bring powerful change to your church—if that's really what you want. Change is a touchy subject that gets mixed reviews, depending on which end of the transformation you are standing on. If you like the way things are going, you might agree with Feodor Dostoevski, who said change is "what people fear most."[1] Even if things aren't going all that great, you might worry that change will make them go from bad to worse. If you're pushing for a revolution, you might agree with John F. Kennedy, who said, "Change is the law of life. And those who look only to the past or the present are certain to miss the future."[2] Both of these extremes (and everything in between) are probably represented in your organization. And when people are passionate about their positions, there are only two fundamental alternatives: negotiation or war. So what's a leader to do?

Listening is the one thing that can bring these diametrically opposed extremes together. Strangely enough, though, it is something passionate resisters and fervent advocates of change both have great difficulty doing. Advocates are afraid listening will slow down the train that leads to progress. Resisters fear that listening will speed up the train and they'll be run over. But without listening, there can be no genuine give-and-take and no mutually agreeable resolution.

The impatient advocates are right about listening slowing things down—in the short term, listening does cause the train to decelerate. They are also wrong because taking the time to understand the concerns that are driving the resistance is usually essential to clearing the tracks for change. So in their own way, the resisters are right about listening speeding things up. But what resisters often fail to realize is this: If their goal is to preserve something they genuinely value, they stand a much better chance if they allow mutual understanding to move forward. The damaging conflict that comes from *not* listening may destroy the stability they cherish as much or more than any change they might fight to prevent.

As we consider change, the natural leadership temperaments and listening styles we've been discussing also enter in, confusing matters and making negotiation even more difficult. Leaders who are energized by fundamentally different aspects of God's work tend to maximize what motivates them and minimize what's important to others. The dynamic tension between the Commander's ongoing crusade for strategic impact, the Performer's perpetual dedication to creating inspirational experiences, the Scholar's unending zeal for pure truth, and the Parent's constant devotion to harmony creates a powerful force within the organization—powerfully good or powerfully bad.

When all of these crucial functions are *in balance*, the church functions like the body of a finely tuned athlete. We can overcome great obstacles and persevere in the race God has marked out for us (Hebrews 12:1). Watch balanced congregations, and you will see inspired disciples who apply Christ's truth in their lives, have great strategic impact in their communities, and genuinely love one another! In this vibrantly healthy church, all seven circles of caring community will be evident. On the other hand, when we allow a single leadership temperament (our own or someone else's) to dominate while others are ignored, even outside observers will see the evidence of perpetual dysfunction.

A runner who has weakness in one leg is said to favor that leg. That's because the stronger leg and the rest of the body have to compensate. Muscles and tendons begin to shape themselves in unhealthy and unnatural configurations that can permanently impair performance. Wise runners who want to win future races will do whatever it takes to strengthen the weakened leg before permanent damage and bad habits set in. If a correction isn't made quickly, these unhealthy configurations quickly start to feel familiar, natural, and even like the best ways to operate. This can also happen in our churches. Without realizing what's happening, as we run the race set before us, we allow certain strengths and passions to dominate in ways that make it harder to overcome obstacles and win the race.

Over time, many leaders become increasingly blind to signs that might reveal the unbalanced tendencies that hinder church growth. It's like gaining weight; it happens slowly, and you get used to the lack of energy and the body aches that come with carrying around twenty extra pounds of cargo. But if you go to the doctor, you are likely to hear that it's time to go on a diet and get some exercise. The doctor may even tell you that those extra pounds you've learned to ignore and live with are actually life threatening. As a leader, imagine yourself as the weight-loss patient. If you listen to what God's Word says about listening (the doctor's orders) and actually do it, you will not only lower your church's risk of untimely death but probably also see tremendous benefits to your congregation's overall health.

Listening to Your Body

We are about to suggest a different kind of listening that can help move change forward in your church—at a pace that's not so slow that it will cause you to miss the opportunities God has for you or so fast that it threatens to destroy the stability God has built so far. To set the stage for this discussion, we need to examine a distinctive leadership model described in Scripture. It is much more organic and less hierarchal or mechanical than the models many of us have been taught. It will probably sound very familiar, but Paul's teaching on Christian leadership is perhaps the most instructive and least heeded by many of today's churches and mission organizations. First Corinthians 12:14-19 says:

> Now the body is not made up of one part but of many. If the foot should say, "Because I am not a hand, I do not belong to the body," it would not for that reason cease to be part of the body. And if the ear should say, "Because I am not an eye, I do not belong to the body," it would not for that reason cease to be part of the body. If the whole body were an eye, where would the sense of hearing be? If the whole body were an ear, where would the sense of smell be? But in fact God has arranged the parts in the body, every one of them, just as he wanted them to be. If they were all one part, where would the body be?

Paul warns us here against a serious trap Christian leaders often fall into. In spite of what we know about God, we act as though God's leadership hierarchy is the same as those we see in human politics or business. In politics or business, the more important you are, the more pay, perks, and respect you deserve. From top to bottom, it's like Old Testament times: first the king, then the nobles, the merchants, the peasants, and finally, lowest of all, the slaves. The modern-day church equivalent of this hierarchy should sound very familiar, and it goes like this: first the senior pastor, then the key leaders (who are more important than the support staff), support staff (who in turn are more valuable than volunteers), and so on. From time to time, kings (or senior pastors) are deposed and replaced by monarchs more agreeable to the nobles (key leaders).

> In spite of what we know about God, we act as though God's leadership hierarchy is the same as those we see in human politics or business.

In Old Testament times, when a king wanted to make a change, he would pray, listen to his royal counselors, consult the nobles, then issue a proclamation that everyone had to obey under pain of death. Those were the good old days! Well, not exactly. Those were also the days of idolatry and infighting and falling away from God. The New Testament ushered in a wonderful leadership change.

Under the new covenant (still in effect today), there is still a king at the top. But the new king is not a fallible, sinful man like Saul or David; it is the Lord. After that the New Testament organizational chart flattens out dramatically. Every Christian is a crown prince and a "joint heir" with Jesus, as Galatians 4:7 tells us. We are no longer slaves but sons, and since we are sons, God has also made us his heirs. Women as well as men are accorded the full inheritance traditionally reserved for sons. There is no distinction between male or female, Jew or Greek, slave or free. We *all* have reserved places of honor in our Father's house and at his table. But what good is it to be a prince or princess if there are no servants? When we issue orders, who will jump up and carry them out?

The other princes and princesses will, of course. For in God's kingdom, we are all royalty, and we are all servants. We are a royal family of servants who wash one another's feet (John 13:12-14), who honor one another above ourselves (Romans 12:10), and who serve one another in love (Galatians 5:13). To the extent that we are obeying God, we are all leaders and worker bees at the same time. There is no honor too high or service too low for the adopted sons and daughters of God. We are all one unit, one body, called to reign with Jesus and work together to do whatever the divine head of our body requires.

We need not climb any ladders to status and success. We also do not need to covet the gifts and temperaments of others who serve in different ways. In the body of Christ, it's good for the eye to be an eye, a foot to be a foot, and an ear to be an ear. This brings us to another big stumbling block Paul warns us against: In spite of what we know about the interdependence of the body, we act as though some parts can function alone.

As we discussed in the last chapter, even the most outstanding leaders may be tempted to ignore or undervalue the contributions of those whose temperaments differ from their own. Society tells us to focus on our strengths, but in the case of the body of Christ, that's not really healthy advice. Paul counters, "On the contrary, those parts of the body that seem to be weaker are indispensable" (1 Corinthians 12:22). As we've said, runners who focus on their strengths and ignore their weaknesses are likely to end up permanently lame.

If we look at leadership in earthly terms, it makes sense to specialize. Successful corporations market their product to niche markets, so why not churches? In an effort to fill the niches we perceive in the Christian community, somehow we miss the absurdity in Paul's image of a body dominated by a single part. Imagine, if you will, "the church of the disembodied eye" (a hit with teenage horror fans) or "the fellowship of the severed ear" (a favorite of Vincent van Gogh enthusiasts). Sounds absurd, doesn't it?

To put it in the terms we've been using in this book, Christians separate and gather in Army churches led by Commanders, Party churches led by Performers, School churches led by Scholars, or Family churches led by Parent leaders. Although each leadership temperament has wonderful strengths, without the balancing influence of the head and the rest of the body, the church can't stay healthy or accomplish the purpose for which it was created.

In his excellent book *Natural Church Development,* Christian Schwarz echoes this theme and uses an illustration of a rain barrel to make his point. He says when a cask is made up of multiple barrel staves of different lengths, the shortest stave, not the longest, will determine how much life-giving water the barrel will hold.[3] In other words, your church can have a spectacular Commander or an amazing Performer, but if you lack the fellowship connections fostered by a Parent leader or the passion for truth the Scholar leader provides, you will be only as strong as your weakest area.

Listening to Your Body's Spiritual Vital Signs

When you go to the hospital, the first thing the medical staff does (after taking your insurance information) is quickly take your physical vital signs. They listen to your heartbeat and breathing and check your temperature and blood pressure. Paying close attention to these four simple indicators gives the medical staff a clear snapshot of how well your body's life-sustaining systems are functioning. If just one system is too high or too low, it's a warning signal that the whole body's wellbeing may be at risk.

As we've mentioned in earlier chapters, four major areas of spiritual health align with the passions of the four leadership temperaments:

❚ The Commander leads people to serve God.

■ The Performer leads people to praise God.

■ The Scholar leads people to know God.

■ The Parent nurtures God's family.

As we've said repeatedly, when all four of these areas of spiritual health are strong and in dynamic balance, a church body will grow and thrive. If just one is unhealthy, the whole body will be out of balance. But how can we listen and discern the health of a church body?

EMI has developed a Spiritual Vital Signs Inventory (p. 193-197) you can use to check on your church's health. There are three ways you can use it to listen to your congregation's perception of its strengths and weaknesses. First, you can photocopy the inventory and complete it yourself to see how you perceive your church's health in these four vital areas.

Second, you can give photocopies to your board of elders, ministry leaders, or some other group of people involved in various aspects of your work. By adding up their scores in the four areas, you can average them to get a group score.

Third, and perhaps most important, you can ask a random sampling of your members to fill out the inventory anonymously and return it to you. Again, add up all of their scores in the four areas and average them to get a group score. The results may surprise you. This is a unique way for leaders to hear how others perceive the health of each aspect of the congregation. Often, perceptions are very different!

Church Personality Profiles

For the last five years, leaders have used the Spiritual Vital Signs Inventory as a concrete way to listen for the health and balance of their churches. They've been excited by the insights they gained. Entire churches (not just leaders) have benefited from dialogues that have taken place as a result of completing the inventory. As they've taken a hard look at themselves, many have realized that their churches, as well as their leaders, fit into one of the four temperaments we've discussed. Since every church has a unique profile and will see unique results, we won't attempt to spell out all the possibilities here. We will, however, touch on some of the basic tendencies of ministries that are overbalanced toward each of the four areas.

▮▮ The Army Church: Focus on Serving God

The driving force behind army-oriented churches and organizations is outward-focused action and impact. These organizations aggressively recruit and mobilize members to serve as foot soldiers to move out into the community with Christ's message of hope and compassion. In addition to sharing the message, the army church often offers practical help such as food, shelter, and job training.

In army churches, there is a passionate determination to achieve tangible, visible results. Army churches are often highly innovative and single-minded. This puts the army church under intense time pressure to recruit fresh volunteers and get them to the front lines to keep up with overwhelming needs. Every organization needs this fire of determination.

The temptation for organizations in intense army mode is burning out the workers. Staff and volunteer leaders too often end up being treated as a regrettably expendable resource. Urgency drives the action. The need is always overwhelming, and the workers are too few. If there is any practical equipping for staff and volunteers, it is generally brief and rarely adequate. Leaders are constantly on the lookout for warm, willing bodies to draft into service. Gary Sweeten, one of EMI's founders who grew up in the Baptist church, suggests that the motto of the army church could be "dip 'em and draft 'em!" (Baptize them and put them to work.)

Does this sound familiar? If so, you are probably personally acquainted with a church or organization that is overbalanced toward the army approach. For a quick application, use the scale below to rate your current leadership situation. A score of five indicates a high likelihood—you're in the army now! A score of one indicates that your troops aren't mobilized—this is probably not your church.

Low	1	2	3	4	5	High

▮▮ The Party Church: Focus on Praising God

The driving force behind party-oriented churches and organizations is providing compelling experiences. These can involve music, public exercise of charismatic gifts, drama, dance, storytelling, and many diverse forms of worship. Strong emphasis is placed on talent. In the party church, you can expect high-quality public speaking, top-notch musical performances, and entertaining skits that use humor to put the audience at ease. Party churches are great at creating emotionally and spiritually gripping programs that keep members and visitors talking all week long.

Excellence and creativity are worthy values in the church setting. After all, who wants to go to another boring church service? The temptation here is to over-focus on experience. Members of party churches may sit passively and give a thumbs up or thumbs down to each service based on how they feel about it. Many of the fastest growing churches in the United States are party-style churches with a strong element of this high-opportunity, low-demand approach. Sometimes, however, these churches are so user-friendly that some of the more demanding elements of discipleship and community become optional extras.

Dave, who also comes from a church background that emphasizes adult baptism, suggests that the motto of these churches could easily be "dip 'em and dazzle 'em!" Use the scale below to rate your current leadership situation. A score of five indicates a high likelihood—join the party! A score of one indicates that in your church, the celebration hasn't started yet.

Low	1	2	3	4	5	High

▌▌▌ The School Church: Focus on Knowing God

The primary passion of the school-oriented church or organization is digging into and expounding on the truth. "Getting it right," being 100 percent faithful to God's Word, is important. Expository preaching and top-quality scholarship reign here. If you attend a meeting at a school church or organization, you are likely to come away with a detailed outline and perhaps even an annotated bibliography! In-depth Bible study, Bible teaching, and doctrinal purity are encouraged among the adults. Children's Sunday school is also a high priority for the school church. In our view, school-oriented churches probably account for nearly 75 percent of American congregations. In many ways, this is the traditional American church.

Again, providing good preaching and sound scholarship is an admirable goal. All of us like to know we're hearing the real deal in our church's Bible and doctrinal teaching. In an age of sound bites and spin, it's refreshing to find depth and faithfulness in getting at the truth. On the down side, these organizations are prone to legalism if they become out of balance. They can talk a good show while tacitly promoting a Pharisaical culture in which knowing and saying the right things are more important than acting in truly Christlike ways. This may lead to a lack of genuineness and cause members to hide problems from one another.

School-oriented churches aim to "sprinkle 'em and straighten 'em out." Their goal is to indoctrinate and maintain proper beliefs and behavior. These inward-focused groups work to maintain the people they already have. They tend to avoid the pressures and potential messes brought into the school by new students who don't know and respect the rules. Outreach is something they talk about but usually leave to poorly paid professionals in denominational or parachurch mission groups. Because of this exclusivity, many school churches have declined in membership.

Use the scale below to rate your current leadership situation. A score of five indicates a high likelihood—class is starting; don't be late! A score of one indicates that your church has missed the school bus.

Low	1	2	3	4	5	High

▌▌▌ The Family Church: Focus on Belonging

The second most common church model we see is Christian organizations or congregations that resemble a big family. The family church is a place where everybody knows your name. In the family church, you know people will pray for you and help you out in times of trouble. The pastor visits your grandma when she's sick and helps you get counseling for your kids when they get in trouble. It's a community in which you both give to and receive from people in personal ways.

Comforting and traditions involving food (and lots of it!), friends, and family make this church a very appealing place to settle in. Roots and loyalties run deep. Every year you know what to expect on Christmas, Easter, and Mother's Day. The pace of change is generally slow, and every member is known.

Family church leaders may be tempted to avoid the pain associated with growth. This church tends to avoid necessary confrontations, smooth over conflicts, and sweep many serious problems under the rug—so be very careful where you walk! All the great things about families are found in these churches. Unfortunately, all of the hard things are present as well. Families argue, and so do these churches. Family churches are often prone to squabbles and power struggles. Because they are so inwardly focused and averse to growth, they often literally become family concerns, with a few families vying for influence and playing Tug of War over resources.

If we had to come up with a motto for this church's leaders, it would be "dip 'em and diaper 'em." In many cases, quite a few members will sit back, relax, and let a minority of responsible, grown-up leaders do the heavy spiritual chores. When these members aren't happy or well-fed, or when things start to smell bad, they will tend to make a lot of noise!

Use the scale below to rate your current leadership situation. A score of five indicates a high likelihood—welcome to the church family reunion! A score of one indicates that your church probably isn't a family affair.

Low	1	2	3	4	5	High

Discovering Your Church's Orientation

Our Spiritual Vital Signs Inventory spiritual profile chart categorizes a congregation's strengths and weaknesses to help you understand your church's specific orientation. Are you inwardly or outwardly focused? Are you more concerned with doing or being? Do you put more of your energies toward loving and serving God or toward loving and serving people?

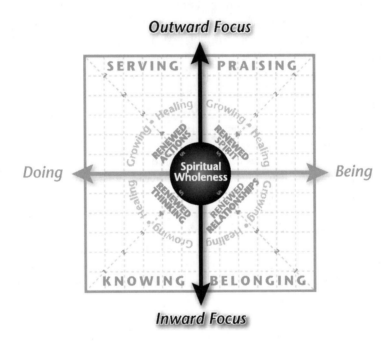

■■■ Inward or Outward?

The *vertical axis* represents people orientation and answers the question "Is the church or leader's primary orientation *inward* or *outward?*" Churches with an inward orientation dig deep with God and one another. They emphasize personal growth and interpersonal connectedness over numerical growth and impact in the larger community. Churches with an outward orientation focus on connecting with people outside of their membership. As a result, outward churches tend to grow faster numerically, and inward churches tend to grow deeper relationally.

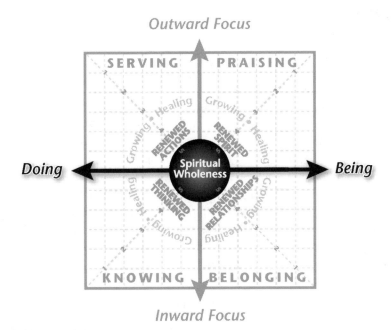

▐▐▐ Doing or Being?

The *horizontal axis* represents action orientation and answers the question "Is the church or leader's primary orientation *doing* or *being*?" In this case, *doing* means having a bias toward taking action on behalf of God and others, and *being* means having a predisposition toward receiving action from God and others.

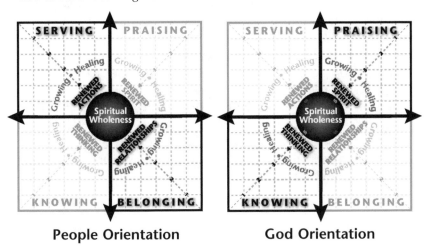

People Orientation   **God Orientation**

▌▌▌ God or People?

Is the church or leader's primary orientation loving and serving *people* or loving and serving *God?* A church with a people orientation will focus its outreach and fellowship programs primarily on meeting human needs. A church with a God orientation will be more concerned with knowing and praising God than with serving people.

As you look at these axes, you'll realize that in addition to understanding their temperament, churches may benefit from understanding their orientation. Each of the four temperaments (army, party, school, family) tends to answer the orientation questions in a particular way. Churches may have a primary and secondary temperament, just as individual leaders do. Depending on how they choose to answer the orientation questions, churches may identify themselves as "school/family," "army/party," "party/family," and so on. Let's take a closer look at the orientation questions now.

▌▌▌ Inward vs. Outward Focus

The Scholar (school church) and Parent (family church) temperaments fall on the inward side of this divide, and the Commander (army church) and Performer (party church) temperaments fall on the outward side.

The *school/family combination* is by far the most common among traditional denominational churches. Although there are exceptions, as time goes by, these churches tend to grow smaller and more exclusive. Because of their intense inward focus, they are also very susceptible to losing members in painful doctrinal and interpersonal splits.

Due to their focus on outreach and experiential worship, churches with an *army/party combination* tend to attract many new people, especially the broken and needy. Army/party churches are unusually good at gathering and inspiring crowds but have difficulties keeping things going on an interpersonal level. Since discipleship and authentic community are generally weak, these churches tend to have a "revolving door" through which large numbers of anonymous people come in and out.

▌▌▌ Doing vs. Being

The Performer (party church) and Parent (family church) fall on the *being* side of this divide, and the Commander (army church) and Scholar (school church) fall on the *doing* side.

Hurting people are often drawn to the charisma they sense from churches with the *party/family combination.* Because there is a strong convergence between healing experiences and healing relationships, these churches are also quite often charismatic in a theological sense. The party/family church is a very accepting place where people can come as they are and be loved. But without strong emphasis on serving and discipleship, the broken people who come often stay that way.

Churches with the *army/school combination* are very serious about doing God's work, both inwardly in their spiritual lives and outwardly in their community. These churches frequently focus a good deal of teaching on the practice of spiritual disciplines such as daily quiet times, devotional reading, intercessory prayer, and tithing. Army/school churches also may emphasize members' responsibilities to evangelize, feed the poor, and help the needy. Because it has so many expectations, the army/school church often unintentionally nudges its members toward legalistic compliance. When the requirements seem too great, members may also hypocritically pretend to comply with the church's multitude of expectations.

▌▌▌ God vs. People

Of course, all churches exist to serve God and people. But in reality, our resources are rarely equally divided between these two important tasks. The *army/family combination* comes down on the people side. This type of church excels at identifying and meeting a wide variety of physical and emotional needs. The people passionately work to bring hope, healing, and connection to Christian and non-Christian alike. God is part of the picture, but the army/family church's focus is on what God can do to help people. Churches with this focus must be wary of missing God's higher purpose as they work to alleviate the pain caused by our fallen human condition.

On the other side of the diagonal, the *school/party combination* trains people to inwardly meditate on and outwardly worship the

Lord. School/party churches encourage the monastic disciplines of solitude, journaling, and deep meditation on Scripture. They also tend to spend long hours in celebration and worship. School/party churches are often in danger of becoming "so heavenly minded that they're no earthly good."

The Spiritual Vital Signs Inventory can be a source of much healthy discussion in your church. As you discover how people perceive your church's strengths and weaknesses, you can begin listening to each other answer the question "How does God want us to grow stronger and healthier?"

By now, you probably recognize your church's need to practice the skills of quick-to-listen leadership. To get where you need to go, all of the leaders with whom you serve need to listen proactively instead of reactively or passively. To break out of unhealthy habits and overcome congregational weaknesses, everyone in your church has to be able to communicate genuine caring, authentic understanding, and Christlike respect. People must learn to confront one another and be immediate. They need to face their own unique temperaments and learn to value the temperaments of others.

We all have to learn to listen for a higher purpose—to become the genuine, Christlike community God intends. That's what our final chapter addresses.

ENDNOTES

1. Eugene E. Brussell, ed., *Webster's New World Dictionary of Quotable Definitions* (New York, NY: Simon & Schuster, Inc., 1988), 72.

2. E. Ehrlitch and M. De Bruhl, *The International Thesaurus of Quotations* (New York, NY: HarperCollins Publishers, Inc., 1996), 80.

3. Christian A. Schwarz, *Natural Church Development: A Guide to Eight Essential Qualities of Healthy Churches* (Carol Stream, IL: ChurchSmart Resources, 1996), 53.

Spiritual Vital Signs Inventory©

Use the Spiritual Vital Signs Inventory on the following pages to help you examine your congregation's strengths and weaknesses in four primary areas of spiritual growth. There are no right or wrong answers to the questions. Since this inventory is designed to help you perceive your congregation's progress on the journey toward greater spiritual wholeness, honesty is all that is required.

Rate your responses using the following scale. Half points are permissible.

1 = disagree

2 = mostly disagree

3 = agree somewhat

4 = mostly agree

5 = agree strongly

▪▪▪ Knowing God

I believe that the majority of the people who've attended our church for a year or more

1. consistently and intentionally set aside quiet time to be alone with God.

Low **1**　　**2**　　**3**　　**4**　　**5** High

2. consistently and intentionally set aside time for personal Bible reading as a way of drawing closer to God.

Low **1**　　**2**　　**3**　　**4**　　**5** High

3. consistently and intentionally set aside private time to give their concerns and anxieties to God in prayer, confession, and worship.

Low **1**　　**2**　　**3**　　**4**　　**5** High

4. consistently and intentionally set aside private time to meditate on Scripture and listen for God's personal guidance for their lives.

Low **1**　　**2**　　**3**　　**4**　　**5** High

5. consistently and intentionally set aside time to write down what God has been teaching them as a way of reinforcing what they've learned.

Low **1**　　**2**　　**3**　　**4**　　**5** High

When you finish responding to the five statements in this section, add the numbers, write your total on the *total* line below, and divide by five to get your *average.*

Total _____

Average _____

▌▌▌ Serving God

I believe that the majority of those who regularly attend our church

1. are regularly and enthusiastically seeking practical ways to serve God inside or outside of the church.

Low **1**   **2**   **3**   **4**   **5** High

2. are presently using (or seeking to discover how to use) their unique spiritual gifts to serve God.

Low **1**   **2**   **3**   **4**   **5** High

3. are presently equipped (or being equipped) to use their spiritual gifts to serve God effectively.

Low **1**   **2**   **3**   **4**   **5** High

4. are being mentored or are mentoring others to become effective in using their spiritual gifts.

Low **1**   **2**   **3**   **4**   **5** High

5. are currently training and releasing others to serve God using their spiritual gifts.

Low **1**   **2**   **3**   **4**   **5** High

When you finish responding to the five statements in this section, add the numbers, write your total on the *total* line below, and divide by five to get your *average*.

Total _____

Average _____

▌▌▌ Praising God

I believe that the majority of those who attend our church

1. regularly experience heartfelt joy and a vibrant sense of God's presence in corporate worship.

Low **1**   **2**   **3**   **4**   **5** High

2. typically feel free and uninhibited in their expressions of praise to God in corporate worship.

Low **1**   **2**   **3**   **4**   **5** High

3. regularly celebrate and publicly give thanks to God for the fruits of answered prayer in their lives.

Low **1**   **2**   **3**   **4**   **5** High

4. usually experience a profound sense of awe and reverence for God's majesty in corporate worship.

Low **1**   **2**   **3**   **4**   **5** High

5. typically leave corporate worship experiences with renewed energy for serving God.

Low **1**   **2**   **3**   **4**   **5** High

When you finish responding to the five statements in this section, add the numbers, write your total on the *total* line below, and divide by five to get your *average*.

Total _____

Average _____

▋▋▋ Belonging to the Family of God

I believe that the majority of those who attend our church

1. feel genuinely accepted, valued, and understood by others in our church community.

Low **1**   **2**   **3**   **4**   **5** High

2. feel safe in sharing deep personal needs and struggles with others in our church community.

Low **1**   **2**   **3**   **4**   **5** High

3. regularly receive and give emotional and practical support to others in our church community.

Low **1**   **2**   **3**   **4**   **5** High

4. often get and give helpful spiritual encouragement to others in our church community.

Low **1**   **2**   **3**   **4**   **5** High

5. speak the truth in love and allow others to help them be accountable to growth goals.

Low **1**   **2**   **3**   **4**   **5** High

When you finish responding to the five statements in this section, add the numbers, write your total on the *total* line below, and divide by five to get your *average*.

Total _____

Average _____

Charting Your Congregation's Spiritual Profile

The chart below has four quadrants marked "Knowing," "Serving," "Praising," and "Belonging." Plot the averages from pages 194-197 by drawing a dot on the diagonal line for each of the four quadrants of the chart. Connect the dots to make a four-sided figure.

Knowing _____

Serving _____

Praising _____

Belonging _____

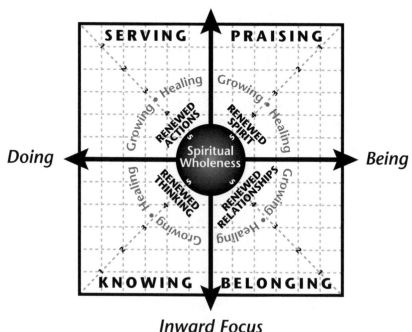

Scoring the Spiritual Vital Signs Inventory for Congregations

▌▌▌ Interpreting Your Spiritual Profile

The closer the shape you have drawn approaches the center of the chart, the greater the wholeness your congregation is likely to be experiencing in that area. The circle formed at about the midpoint of each section indicates specific areas of growing and healing. If your average is in an area that is outside that circle, your congregation is probably feeling some sense of disconnection or need for growth in the indicated area. If your average is inside the circle, you are likely to be experiencing a growing sense of wholeness and healing in that area.

▌▌▌ Inward vs. Outward Focus

Next compare the top two quadrants marked "Outward Focus" and the bottom two quadrants marked "Inward Focus." The farther away the plot points are from the center of the graph in the Serving and Praising areas, the greater your congregation's need for growth in the outward or public dimensions of their relationships with God. The farther away the plot points are from the center of the graph in the Knowing and Belonging areas, the greater your congregation's need for growth in the inward and more private dimensions of their relationships with God. It is important to realize that inward and outward expressions of our faith are both essential to spiritual wholeness.

Churches that are outwardly focused will tend to grow numerically. Churches that are inwardly focused will tend to experience greater depth of relationship with God and with others. True wholeness and maturity require both.

▌▌▌ Doing vs. Being

The left two quadrants are marked "Doing." They reflect the tendency toward an action-oriented spirituality that expresses itself in consistently developing and practicing spiritual habits that promote deeper relationships and obedience to God's desires for your life.

The right two quadrants are marked "Being." They reflect a tendency toward receiving-oriented spirituality that expresses itself in experiencing deep emotional and spiritual support through both worship and personal relationships.

The farther away the plot points are from the center of the graph in the Serving and Knowing areas, the greater the need to become more active and intentional in pursuing spiritual goals. On the other hand, the farther away the plot points are from the center of the graph in the Praising and Belonging areas, the greater your congregation's need to learn how to more fully receive and experience practical and spiritual support from God and from people. It is important to realize that doing and being are both essential aspects of spiritual wholeness.

■■■ Best Use of the Spiritual Vital Signs Inventory

The Spiritual Vital Signs Inventory is most helpful when used in a relational context. You'll obtain the best results and insights when you share your inventory with both lay people and leaders in your congregation. Discussing growing edges, setting goals, encouraging each other, and praying together forms an effective and rewarding pathway to congregational growth. May God bless you as you seek to follow him and receive all he has for your church.

If you have any questions or comments about the use of this inventory, please call Equipping Ministries International at 1-800-EMI-GROW (364-4769).

Spiritual Vital Signs Inventory Reflection Questions

The balance between quadrants on the Spiritual Vital Signs Inventory can give you great insight into what your congregation is currently experiencing, but remember that you and God are the final authorities on determining your actual needs. With that in mind, you'll want to take some time to consider and discuss your church's profile. The following pages provide important reflection questions that will help you decide what may be hindering you from experiencing more of the wholeness God intends for your church.

There are two basic barriers to consider in each area of your spiritual life: barriers of attitude and barriers of opportunity. Attitude barriers are the false inner beliefs, excuses, or self-talk that we use to explain why we can't have the abundant life Jesus promises in John 10:10. These false beliefs must be identified so we can move beyond them and experience wholeness. If you need help identifying false beliefs, consider attending EMI's "Renewing the Mind" course for additional help in this area. Barriers of opportunity are external factors or physical problems that get in the way of ministry.

▮▮▮ Knowing God ▮▮▮

The area of knowing God focuses on the private actions you can take to deepen your relationship with God. This includes taking private time alone with God, individual prayer, devotional Bible reading, personal study, listening for God's voice, seeking God's guidance, applying Christlike principles in daily decisions, and spiritual journaling.

Among other things, Scripture indicates that God desires that we learn to

▮ seek him in private (Matthew 6:6);

▮ hide his Word in our hearts (Psalm 119:11);

▮ lay down our burdens, learn from him, and find rest for our souls (Matthew 11:28-29);

▮ use his Word to test the thoughts and attitudes of our hearts (Hebrews 4:12); and

▮ use his Word to prepare for good works (2 Timothy 2:15; 3:16).

▮▮▮ Barriers: Attitudes About Knowing God

What specific beliefs or attitudes might currently be hindering your congregation's growth in this area?

What renewed beliefs or attitudes are likely to produce growth toward greater wholeness in this area?

▮▮▮ Barriers: Opportunities for Knowing God

What factors currently limit opportunity for your congregation's growth toward greater wholeness in this area?

What are some practical steps you might take to increase opportunity for growth in this area?

▌▌▌ Serving God ▌▌▌

This area focuses on outward acts of obedience that demonstrate our relationship with God. This is usually accomplished through identifying and utilizing our unique spiritual gifts, talents, and skills to help accomplish the overall mission of the body of Christ.

Among other things, Scripture indicates that God desires that we serve

▌ with enthusiasm (1 Peter 5:2b; Ephesians 6:7),

▌ by eagerly seeking spiritual gifts that build up the church (1 Corinthians 14:12),

▌ by passionately working to improve in using our gifts (1 Timothy 4:14-15),

▌ by using whatever gifts we have received to bless others (1 Peter 4:10), and

▌ by multiplying ourselves through mentoring and teaching others (2 Timothy 2:2).

▌▌▌ Barriers: Attitudes About Serving God

What specific beliefs or attitudes might currently be hindering your congregation's growth in this area?

What renewed beliefs or attitudes are likely to produce growth toward greater wholeness in this area?

▌▌▌ Barriers: Opportunities for Serving God

What factors currently limit opportunity for your congregation's growth toward greater wholeness in this area?

What are some practical steps you might take to increase opportunity for growth in this area?

▌▌▌ Praising God ▌▌▌

The area of praising God focuses on outward acts of corporate praise, adoration, and reverence toward God as well as celebration of various aspects of our relationship with him. This is usually accomplished through public testimonies of praise and thanksgiving, music, singing, corporate prayer, or silent reflection.

Among other things, Scripture indicates that God desires that we worship

- ▌ and rejoice in the hope of his glory (Romans 5:2);

- ▌ with all of our hearts, by reciting his wonders, and by singing his praise (Psalm 9:1-2);

- ▌ by sharing our Master's joy and happiness at our redemption (Matthew 25:21);

- ▌ by joining with the angels in joyful exaltation (Hebrews 12:22-23); and

- ▌ by being thankful and approaching him with reverence and awe (Hebrews 12:28-29).

▌▌▌ Barriers: Attitudes About Praising God

What specific beliefs or attitudes might currently be hindering your congregation's growth in this area?

What renewed beliefs or attitudes are likely to produce growth toward greater wholeness in this area?

▌▌▌ Barriers: Opportunities for Praising God

What factors currently limit opportunity for your congregation's growth toward greater wholeness in this area?

What are some practical steps you might take to increase opportunity for growth in this area?

▋▋▋ Belonging to God's Family ▋▋▋

This area focuses on our personal experience of relationship with God through close interpersonal connection with others within the family of God. This is usually accomplished through developing warm, committed, Christlike friendships in which we can give and receive encouragement, practical support, and accountability in reaching spiritual growth goals.

Among other things, Scripture indicates that God desires that we

▋ devote ourselves to fellowship, breaking bread, and prayer (Acts 2:42);

▋ support his people who are in need (Romans 12:13);

▋ share our joys and suffering as part of the body of Christ (1 Corinthians 12:26-27);

▋ receive special care as one who belongs to the family of believers (Galatians 6:10); and

▋ love our brothers and sisters in Christ (1 Peter 2:17).

▋▋▋ Barriers: Attitudes About Belonging to God's Family

What specific beliefs or attitudes might currently be hindering your congregation's growth in this area?

What renewed beliefs or attitudes are likely to produce growth toward greater wholeness in this area?

▋▋▋ Barriers: Opportunities for Belonging to God's Family

What factors currently limit opportunity for your congregation's growth toward greater wholeness in this area?

What are some practical steps you might take to increase opportunity for growth in this area?

"Listen, my dear brothers: Has not God chosen those who are poor in the eyes of the world to be rich in faith and to inherit the kingdom he promised those who love him?" (James 2:5).

12

Blessings of
LISTENING

One morning at the height of his public popularity, Jesus looked out over the clamoring crowd that surrounded him. Countless family groups who'd walked or limped or been carried innumerable miles waited to hear his teaching, desperately hoping they'd be healed from their diseases or delivered from their demons. Crowds had become a common enough sight for Jesus and his growing band of disciples; but today would be special. Although he spoke to the crowd, this teaching focused on his disciples, that little band of leadership trainees who would soon turn the world upside down. Jesus knew that before they could become world-changing leaders, they had to take hold of the upside-down secrets of his coming kingdom. Here's how *The Message* translation renders Jesus' words from the Gospel of Matthew 5:1-13:

When Jesus saw his ministry drawing huge crowds, he climbed a hillside. Those who were apprenticed to him, the committed, climbed with him. Arriving at a quiet place, he sat down and taught his climbing companions. This is what he said:

"You're blessed when you're at the end of your rope. With less of you there is more of God and his rule.

"You're blessed when you feel you've lost what is most dear to you. Only then can you be embraced by the One most dear to you.

"You're blessed when you're content with just who you are— no more, no less. That's the moment you find yourselves proud owners of everything that can't be bought.

"You're blessed when you've worked up a good appetite for God. He's food and drink in the best meal you'll ever eat.

"You're blessed when you care. At the moment of being 'care-full,' you find yourselves cared for.

"You're blessed when you get your inside world—your mind and heart—put right. Then you can see God in the outside world.

"You're blessed when you can show people how to cooperate instead of compete or fight. That's when you discover who you really are, and your place in God's family.

"You're blessed when your commitment to God provokes per-secution. The persecution drives you even deeper into God's kingdom."

What Jesus told his disciples must have sounded a little crazy. The words Jesus said and the pictures he painted of how to find blessing and happiness not only didn't match their idea of what the Messiah's kingdom should look like but were its exact opposite.

The eight essential attitudes Jesus talked about that day are now widely known as the Beatitudes. The word *beatitude* literally refers to a beautiful state of ecstasy or heavenly bliss, but Christ's words explain shockingly down-to-earth attitudes and behaviors leaders need for following Jesus. In our ears, they also speak of the biblical DNA required for every quick-to-listen leader.

▮▮▮ Attitude 1: God Is Looking for *Poor* Listeners

"Blessed are the poor in spirit, for theirs is the kingdom of heaven" (Matthew 5:3).

If somewhere along the way, before you picked up this book or as you've been reading it, you've realized that you're not the sensitive, caring, skilled listener God wants you to be, you're blessed. It's only leaders who realize that they don't have all their stuff together that God can use in the life-changing ministry of listening. In his book *The Purpose-Driven Life*, Rick Warren puts it this way: "God has never been impressed with strength or self-sufficiency. In fact, he is drawn to people who are weak and admit it. Jesus regarded this recognition of our need as being *'poor in spirit.'* "[1]

If you are a poor listener, and all of us are from time to time, you will have to learn to step out of your "competence zone" and rely on God to help you grow. In our experience, that's where God meets us most often anyway. As you've read this book and asked others for feedback, you are probably becoming increasingly conscious of your inadequacies as a listener. This means you're already making progress! Coming to grips with how *poor* we really are is a huge step on the path toward the quick-to-listen wisdom of God's kingdom.

The trick is not to give up. In your conversations, consciously listen for feelings and thoughts and begin reflecting them back. With the Holy Spirit's help, you will soon be listening better than you ever thought you could. As you continue to listen with one ear toward heaven and the other toward your listening partner, you will be amazed at the ways God uses your efforts.

This isn't pop psychology; it's basic Christianity. After all, when James wrote about being quick to listen and slow to speak, there weren't any psychologists. So just be a poor listener and do your best to let God use you. The results are always up to him anyway. That leads us to the next attitude.

▮▮▮ Attitude 2: God Is Looking for *Broken-Hearted* Listeners

"Blessed are those who mourn, for they will be comforted" (Matthew 5:4).

Many of our listening students have confessed that they felt too wounded to help anyone else with their struggles. For anyone grieving the loss of an elderly parent, a beloved spouse, or a miscarried child, it's hard to imagine how even God could turn these terrible times of emptiness and despair into a blessing. Most of us remember September 11, 2001, as the tragic day the United States was attacked by terrorists. To Anne, the numbness and shock that followed those strikes were the backdrop for another deeply tragic event.

On the morning of September 13, 2001, I received a phone call from my daughter-in-law, Holly, who was twenty-one weeks pregnant with twins, a little boy and a little girl. She said, "I am not sure if something is going on, but I wonder if you would be willing to go to the doctor with me at noon." I quickly agreed and asked my Bible study group, which was meeting at my home, to pray for Holly. We went to the doctor, expecting a pretty routine visit. But all of a sudden the medical staff began asking if Holly wanted to do everything she could to save the babies. Minutes later we were in an ambulance rushing to a local hospital.

This was Holly's first pregnancy, and she and my son Bill were beside themselves with excitement to become parents of twins. But a severe infection had set in, and the babies were born the following day. We held Ashley and William, prayed for them, and baptized them during their forty-five minutes of life. Pain, emptiness, and helplessness filled all of our hearts but most excruciatingly Bill's and Holly's. They really did not know how they would be able to move on.

Soon, Holly began to hear about many women with similar experiences who were able to share their pain with one another. Attending a "grief support" group at the hospital put Holly and Bill in touch with other young couples that were walking through their pain at the same time. It was a comfort to have others know how they felt and to be free to talk about their grief together.

Holly was eventually asked to be on a hospital panel that would teach the doctors and nurses how to better minister to patients losing babies. As she participated in these gatherings, she was amazed at how much she was helped by the opportunity to help others. She returned home blessed by those who shed tears alongside her as she recalled that terrible experience. She was also blessed by a father on the panel who had lost twins nine months previously and who had not allowed himself to shed a single tear, even though his heart was about to break. As he listened to Holly, the Lord opened the floodgates of his heart and allowed the healing process to continue.

Bill and Holly are now the proud parents of Caroline and her baby sister, Lauren, who are the light of their lives. But they still feel a deep sensitivity to those who have lost babies. Their lives were changed forever by this experience.

The blessing here isn't in the pain or in the loss but in finding something real and true and comforting to light another's way through desolation. The graveyard of mourning is the last place we'd expect to find comfort, but even though it feels empty, it's not. God is especially present here. Though we may not sense God at first, he is at hand and intimately acquainted with our grief. Isaiah 53:4 promises that God will meet us here to take up our infirmities and carry our sorrows. When we pour out the grief and emptiness of our hearts, God listens. God is the only one who genuinely understands and cares about what we're going through even more than we do.

> The blessing here isn't in the pain or in the loss but in finding something real and true and comforting to light another's way through desolation.

God's comfort becomes most real in suffering. Comfort doesn't come from having answers about why things happen the way they do. It comes from being heard and understood. When we've lost someone or something we care about, there aren't a lot of words that will bring comfort. The greatest consolation comes from loving people who are willing to be there and listen. They provide open arms and strong shoulders to cry on when we're ready for them.

Leaders who know what it is to mourn *and* to be comforted have something precious to give. They've had to open up a deep, vulnerable, and frightening place to God and other people—and they've found comfort there. They've discovered that their place of ultimate emptiness *isn't empty after all*. In fact, it's a kind of holy of holies where God dwells most richly in their lives.

Quick-to-listen leaders know from personal experience that this painful place is holy ground. Like Moses, they've learned to take off their shoes and tread lightly around tender hearts. They give their ears quickly and give advice sparingly because they know what mourning feels like. They practice Christlike listening instead of trying to provide answers to unanswerable questions. They rejoice with those who rejoice and mourn with those who mourn, but most all, they're real. They've sworn off quick advice-giving and replaced it with a willingness to walk side by side with the happy and the hurting alike.

▌▌▌ Attitude 3: God Is Looking for *Humble* Listeners

"Blessed are the meek, for they will inherit the earth" (Matthew 5:5).

Meekness in leadership means learning to *listen without having to be in control.* A humble listener is one who knows how to quiet his need to push, pull, or drag others to the place he wants them to be. Henri Nouwen describes the lessons in meekness that he received when he left a prestigious teaching post at Harvard to work with mentally handicapped adults:

> *I still have moments in which I clamp down and tell everyone to shut up, get in line, listen to me, and believe what I say. But I am also getting in touch with the mystery that leadership, for a large part, means to be led.[2]*

Like Nouwen, meek leaders are willing to respect and learn from the people around them without reference to their worldly status. Meekness means taking all the time necessary to discover how others think and feel. According to Jesus, treating people with meekness will eventually put us in possession of the whole earth. How could that possibly be? Doesn't Jesus also want us to fight and vanquish wickedness, selfishness, and corruption? Yes, he does. But the only wickedness we can truly conquer lies within our own hearts. For God's will to be done and his kingdom to come, we must become like Jesus in this critical area. We must have the courage and the patience to be meek.

Meekness is not weakness. On the contrary, it calls on us to battle courageously with natural self-centeredness. For leaders this often means being careful not to enforce our point of view even when it would be easy to do so. It means fighting our prejudices and not jumping to conclusions about people's motives. Most important, meekness means honoring God's terrible and precious gift of free will. Like it or not, we must honor the rights of others to think for themselves, to disagree, and even to make harmful choices that have painful consequences.

▮▮▮ Attitude 4: God Is Looking for *Hungry* Listeners

"Blessed are those who hunger and thirst for righteousness, for they will be filled" (Matthew 5:6).

There is nothing more basic than hunger and thirst. If we do not satisfy our built-in need for food and water, our bodies will shut down and eventually die. Our spiritual hunger seems almost as basic. As we serve others by listening, we will see the Lord work in ways that make us hunger for more. If you've experienced sacred moments when God used you to help his goodness break through into someone else's life, you know how spiritually satisfying it can be. Once you've tasted and seen that the ministry of listening is good, your spiritual stomach will begin to growl and your spiritual mouth will begin to water for more opportunities to share God's grace in this way.

For some of us, it may be hard to imagine being hungry to listen instead of eager to talk. Listening is, after all, an acquired taste. Yet if our food is to do the will of him who sent us (John 4:34), there is a wonderful sustenance to be had by obeying God's inner prompting to listen more and talk less.

Anne's three-year-old grandson Jason's preschool teacher asked him if he knew what the word *obey* means. Without missing a beat, Jason responded, "It means to listen and do." That's the obedience God is asking from us. In listening there are no giant steps, just countless attention-giving baby steps that will lead us to amazingly rich stores of spiritual food. With each baby step, we move closer to loving the Lord our God with all our hearts, souls, and minds and loving our neighbors as ourselves.

The living water of Christ's love flows best in the streambed of community. The righteousness we thirst for is not the painstaking obedience to laws and rituals envisioned by the Pharisees. It's relational. It flows from the Father, Son, and Holy Spirit into us—and through us to others. It also flows from God into others—and through them into us.

▮▮▮ Attitude 5: God Is Looking for *Merciful* Listeners

"Blessed are the merciful, for they will be shown mercy" (Matthew 5:7).

Mercy is a gift—it's not really mercy if you give it just to get something. Mercy isn't something we give because it feels good or even because it's our duty. We freely give the mercy of listening because our Lord and king freely offers it to us. We're completely unworthy of this royal gift, but as Matthew 25:40 says, whatever mercy we show to even the least deserving of our brothers and sisters, it's as if we were giving it directly back to Jesus. When you think of it this way, every moment of our time, every calorie of physical or spiritual energy we burn, every sacrifice we make in the ministry of listening is a true act of worship.

As Mark 4:24-27 indicates, the measure we use in giving mercy to others will be used on us in the end. Mercy is a spiritual outlay that multiplies and grows in us as we give it away. The more generously we show mercy by giving people our time and our ears when they need us, the more our spiritual wealth and capacity to give mercy will grow. On the

> It's not fair, and it's not equitable. That's what makes it merciful.

other hand, if we are stingy with the mercies we give, our spiritual bank account dwindles until we eventually have nothing left to give. The more we hold on to our time and hold back our compassion, the less we will have for ourselves.

Mercy doesn't always feel good in the moment. As leaders, we will frequently have to fight down our annoyance at the inconvenience others' needs impose on our already busy schedules. We will often be required to lay down urgent agendas and postpone important tasks so that God's mercy can flow through us. It's not fair, and it's not equitable. That's what makes it merciful. In the moments you're practicing Christlike listening, you serve as a kind of living water pipe that transfers Christ's undeserved, unearned patience and love to someone else who needs it. Now that's mercy!

▌▌▌ Attitude 6: God Is Looking for *Genuine* Listeners

"Blessed are the pure in heart, for they will see God" (Matthew 5:8).

One of the typical complaints we hear from leaders who are struggling with listening is that they don't *feel genuine* as they practice their listening skills. When we take the time to unpack what they're really saying, we usually find that it's not the skills that are uncomfortable; it's changing the habits they've repeated so often that they've become second nature. The feeling these leaders express is a bit like the discomfort most Americans feel trying to drive in England or India. Driving on the "wrong side of the road" often feels so scary, uncomfortable, and wrong that many Americans give up after trying for only a few minutes. Of course, there is nothing really wrong or inherently bad about driving on a different side of the road or following slightly different traffic laws, but it just doesn't feel right at first.

In the same way, the *feeling* of being genuine and actually *being genuine* are two different things. The real measure of genuineness is not how you feel but the purity of your motives. No matter how relaxed and "authentic" it may feel, poor listening is an indicator of self-focus rather than sincerity. Being pure in heart requires us to concentrate vigilantly on matching our desires and behavior to what God wants, not what we want. So it's not really so surprising that we might see God more when, with pure hearts, we carefully watch and wait for opportunities to do his will.

> The real measure of genuineness is not how you feel but the purity of your motives.

Purity of heart has to be learned and practiced until it transforms us. That's what Paul is talking about in Romans 12:2 when he says, "Do not conform any longer to the pattern of this world, but be transformed by the renewing of your mind." No one starts out pure in heart; we're all sinful and fallen. But we can be transformed by allowing our hearts to be "remodeled" according to God's specifications and not the world's. Though it may feel uncomfortable, especially at first, this remodeling includes things like being slow to speak and quick to listen.

Romans 12:2 ends with this promise: As your natural ways of thinking and behavior are transformed and remodeled in Christlike ways, "you will be able to test and approve what God's will is—his good, pleasing and perfect will." In other words, the more transformed you become, the more you will see God and understand what he really wants. This doesn't mean that any technique we have suggested in this book is the only way for you to become the listening leader God wants you to be. But whether you use these techniques or find others, being pure in heart will require you to exchange your old habits for new ones.

■■■ Attitude 7: God Is Looking for *Compromising* Listeners

"Blessed are the peacemakers, for they will be called sons of God" (Matthew 5:9).

Peacemaking should be the one attitude that no one can disagree with, right? Wrong! Some of you probably read Attitude 7 and thought to yourselves, "Compromise? We can never compromise! Compromise is a slippery slope on the way to liberalism, humanism, and a thousand other evils!" Of course, we're not talking about compromising the truth of Scripture but about listening and speaking the truth in love in a way that allows us to work out interpersonal differences so we can accomplish God's purposes as a harmonious team. Most of us are all for this kind of peacemaking—unless it means we have to change.

It's a fact that no two human beings have exactly the same wants, desires, tastes, and needs. As a result, there is no one-size-fits-all way of doing things that works for everyone. God must have made us this way for a reason, but to leaders charged with helping diverse groups work together, our individuality can feel like a royal pain.

Peacemaking is hard work that starts with acknowledging your own wants and needs, then moves on to listening to the needs and wants of others. Peacemaking ends, whenever possible, with negotiating compromises that allow all parties to come out ahead. Ah, sweet compromise. But in the process, strong emotions and fierce beliefs are triggered. The reactive listening animals we discussed in Chapter 4 are unleashed. Things are said that would be much better unsaid, and things are done that cause deep wounds. We've all been there.

With the best of good intentions, peacemakers try to mediate the Tug of War between opposing perceptions and passionately held positions. You would think people would be more grateful, but when it doesn't look like you're taking their side, suddenly the peacemaker becomes the enemy and both sides attack. Those of us with scars from these unsuccessful peacemaking attempts have learned that the best kind of peacemaking is preventative.

Real peacemaking means handling differences and emotions immediately and being quick to listen well before battle lines are drawn. Peacemakers refuse to gossip or talk about others behind their backs. Instead, they go straight to the people involved and work out relational tension before it builds up. It's like taking care of a leaky roof or an overflowing septic system before serious, irreparable damage is done. Quick-to-listen leaders learn to attend to the regular chores required to maintain harmony in their relationships.

▐▐▐ Attitude 8: God Is Looking for *Courageous* Listeners

"Blessed are those who are persecuted because of righteousness, for theirs is the kingdom of heaven" (Matthew 5:10).

Being a quick-to-listen leader isn't much fun, especially when the time comes to make sure unpopular points of view are heard, to ask tough questions, or to point out discrepancies between what's being said and done. But the body of Christ desperately needs listening leaders who are willing to sacrifice their own comfort to preserve its health, honesty, and integrity. In difficult situations, our job is often to cast unwelcome light into dark corners so we can deal with unpleasant things some would rather not expose.

Many leaders are all too ready to close their eyes, cover their ears, and chant, "La-la-la-la...I can't hear you!" to drown out the rumblings of division and discontent. They've counted the cost of fearless listening and speaking the truth in love and decided not to risk the pain and rejection they might entail. It's natural to want to avoid such pain, but as we all know, it's also very unhealthy. The realities we avoid today contain the tragedies that will destroy us tomorrow.

If you choose to lead, you need to expect that sooner or later you'll be "persecuted for righteousness' sake." It comes with the territory. When you listen proactively and speak the truth in love for Christ's sake (and for the sake of his church), there will always be opposition. In fact, in Matthew 5:11 Jesus says there will be people who'll insult you, harass you, and falsely say all kinds of evil things against you in spite of your best efforts (or perhaps because of them). If you've been in ministry long, you've probably already experienced this painful reality.

So when your motivations are misconstrued or malicious gossip rears its ugly head, stay your course and hold fast to Jesus' promise: "Great is your reward in heaven." And although it may not seem like it in the moment of persecution, the earthly benefits of doing Christ's work for righteousness' sake aren't bad either. Doing right and fearlessly facing the music that comes with it build up God's kingdom. If you persist in listening early and often and fearlessly speaking the truth in love, you'll establish healthy norms that lead to an increasingly Christlike community. Your listening will act as a preventative antibiotic that strengthens your church against all kinds of diseases. It paves the way for innumerable blessings.

Blessed Are the Listeners

The Beatitudes reveal the wonderful upside-down quality that makes God's kingdom so irresistible. They expose things we've always thought of as burdens to be the greatest of blessings. The least are the greatest, and things we thought were huge and insurmountable are nothing to worry about after all. If the Beatitudes are more than just interesting philosophical wordplay (we believe they are, and we hope you do too), the little practical ways we honor God in our daily lives and relationships may ultimately yield the most important treasures we will ever discover. If we could write our own Beatitude, it would say something like "Blessed are the listeners, for they will be heard." The surest way we know to see big results in leadership, discipleship, and even prayer is to cultivate the seemingly minor spiritual discipline of listening.

> Our ministry of listening begets listeners more surely than our most convincing argument ever could.

We've talked a great deal about the benefits of listening and speaking the truth in love to other people. We've talked about how it opens doors of trust and deeper understanding. But for the leader, perhaps one of the most important side-blessings of listening is that it also opens ears to hear what you have to say. When evangelists or teachers talk of "earning the right to be heard," whether they know it or not, they're talking about listening. Teachability and openness to considering new ideas are caught, rather than taught. In other words, our ministry of listening begets listeners more surely than our most convincing argument ever could.

Highly effective disciples are trained by leaders who listen. Instead of merely taking in a mentor's inspiring ideas or learning to execute a leader's brilliant strategies, followers of listening leaders gain something far more valuable: They learn how to love and gain the trust of followers. Since disciples will imitate what their mentors *do* more than what they say, the best way to train teachable followers is to be an open, flexible, tuned-in leader. Leader, if you're not listening, don't be surprised if your followers emulate your bad habits. And if you aren't quick to listen to the people you see and interact with every day, you'll probably have real problems listening to God.

In our first book about listening,[3] we devoted a whole chapter to the practical "how-tos" of hearing God's voice. Since this book is addressed primarily to pastors and leaders, we won't presume to tell you how to get your divine inspiration. Suffice it to say that we think the best ways to hear God are strikingly similar to the best ways to hear people. Being quiet, devoting time, and concentrating your attention go a long way. Whether you focus your listening on Scripture, the circumstances of your life, or the stirrings of your inmost spirit, God is speaking all the time. As Psalm 19:2 says, "Day after day they pour forth speech; night after night they display knowledge." God *is* speaking. Are you listening?

A God Who Listens...and Answers

If your heart is quick and receptive to God's voice and you are able to put aside your own plans long enough to listen, God has wonderful things to show you. You may be working to transform your own church community or to accomplish wonderful works in countries across the world. Whatever your leadership role may be, whether you lead multitudes or a meager few, God has big plans for you. Whether you know it or not, you are chosen.

" 'I know the plans I have for you,' declares the Lord, 'plans to prosper you and not to harm you, plans to give you hope and a future. Then you will call upon me and come and pray to me, and I will listen to you' " (Jeremiah 29:11-12).

If you are truly on God's team, he is rooting for you and working to bless and strengthen you. God wants to give you hope, to equip you for a bright future where you can harmonize your gifts and temperament with the rest of his body. These things are amazing to think about. The God of the universe has a plan—just for you! But that's not all. The most spectacular promise in this verse is contained in the last five words: "I will listen to you." God is quick to listen.

The infinite God, who made the vast reaches of the universe, is intimately interested in and ready to ponder the smallest emotions you're feeling and the biggest leadership questions you're wondering about right now. God's Holy Spirit is constantly listening to you in all the ways we've been talking about and many more. God isn't just looking down in a disinterested way; he's listening closely and ready to answer and reveal himself in exciting ways. Our encouragement to you is to follow his lead. Imitate the listening ways of your heavenly Father, and teach your followers to do the same.

"Prepare God's people for works of service, so that the body of Christ may be built up until we all reach unity in the faith and in the knowledge of the Son of God and become mature, attaining to the whole measure of the fullness of Christ" (Ephesians 4:12-13).

Think about it. What are the true qualities of a mature, Christlike disciple or leader? Twelve simple words from James 1:19 will certainly help us go a long way in the right direction. They are the beginning of a maturity and wisdom that we desperately need in our churches today.

"Be quick to listen, slow to speak and slow to become angry."

ENDNOTES

1. Rick Warren, *The Purpose-Driven Life: What on Earth Am I Here For?* (Grand Rapids, MI: Zondervan, 2002), 273.

2. Henri J. M. Nouwen, *In the Name of Jesus: Reflections on Christian Leadership* (New York, NY: The Crossroad Publishing Company, 1996), 56-57.

3. Gary Sweeten, Dave Ping, and Anne Clippard, *Listening for Heaven's Sake: Building Healthy Relationships With God, Self and Others* (Cincinnati, OH: Teleios Publications, 1993).

"The tongue has the power of life and death"
(Proverbs 18:21a).

"I tell you that men will have to give account on the day of judgment for every careless word they have spoken. For by your words you will be acquitted, and by your words you will be condemned" (Matthew 12:36-37).

SCRIPTURES FOR

Quick-to-Listen LEADERS

■■■ Caring

"Praise the Lord, O my soul, and forget not all his benefits—who forgives all your sins and heals all your diseases, who redeems your life from the pit and crowns you with love and compassion" (Psalm 103:2-4).

"Teacher, which is the greatest commandment in the Law?"

"Jesus replied: ' "Love the Lord your God with all your heart and with all your soul and with all your mind." This is the first and greatest commandment. And the second is like it: "Love your neighbor as yourself." All the Law and the Prophets hang on these two commandments' " (Matthew 22:36-40).

"And I will ask the Father, and he will give you another Counselor to be with you forever—the Spirit of truth" (John 14:16-17a).

"Praise be to the God and Father of our Lord Jesus Christ, the Father of compassion and the God of all comfort, who comforts us in all our troubles, so that we can comfort those in any trouble with the comfort we ourselves have received from God" (2 Corinthians 1:3-4).

"If you have any encouragement from being united with Christ, if any comfort from his love, if any fellowship with the Spirit, if any tenderness and compassion, then make my joy complete by being like-minded, having the same love, being one in spirit and purpose" (Philippians 2:1-2).

"Therefore, as God's chosen people, holy and dearly loved, clothe yourselves with compassion, kindness, humility, gentleness and patience" (Colossians 3:12).

"But encourage one another daily, as long as it is called Today, so that none of you may be hardened by sin's deceitfulness" (Hebrews 3:13).

▮▮▮ Empathy

"The heart of the righteous weighs its answers, but the mouth of the wicked gushes evil" (Proverbs 15:28).

"A fool finds no pleasure in understanding but delights in airing his own opinions" (Proverbs 18:2).

"He who answers before listening—that is his folly and shame" (Proverbs 18:13).

"Do you see a man who speaks in haste? There is more hope for a fool than for him" (Proverbs 29:20).

"The only thing that counts is faith expressing itself through love" (Galatians 5:6b).

"We do not have a high priest who is unable to sympathize with our weaknesses, but we have one who has been tempted in every way, just as we are—yet was without sin" (Hebrews 4:15).

"My dear brothers, take note of this: Everyone should be quick to listen, slow to speak and slow to become angry" (James 1:19).

▮▮▮ Respect

"So God created man in his own image, in the image of God he created him; male and female he created them" (Genesis 1:27).

"You made him a little lower than the heavenly beings and crowned him with glory and honor" (Psalm 8:5).

"When words are many, sin is not absent, but he who holds his tongue is wise" (Proverbs 10:19).

"A man who lacks judgment derides his neighbor, but a man of understanding holds his tongue" (Proverbs 11:12).

"Pleasant words are a honeycomb, sweet to the soul and healing to the bones" (Proverbs 16:24).

"Even a fool is thought wise if he keeps silent, and discerning if he holds his tongue" (Proverbs 17:28).

"A word aptly spoken is like apples of gold in settings of silver" (Proverbs 25:11).

"Like one who takes away a garment on a cold day, or like vinegar poured on soda, is one who sings songs to a heavy heart" (Proverbs 25:20).

"My brothers, as believers in our glorious Lord Jesus Christ, don't show favoritism. Suppose a man comes into your meeting wearing a gold ring and fine clothes, and a poor man in shabby clothes also comes in. If you show special attention to the man wearing fine clothes and say, 'Here's a good seat for you,' but say to the poor man, 'You stand there' or 'Sit on the floor by my feet,' have you not discriminated among yourselves and become judges with evil thoughts?" (James 2:1-4).

"Live as free men, but do not use your freedom as a cover-up for evil; live as servants of God. Show proper respect to everyone: Love the brotherhood of believers, fear God, honor the king" (1 Peter 2:16-17).

"Brothers, if someone is caught in a sin, you who are spiritual should restore him gently. But watch yourself, or you also may be tempted. Carry each other's burdens, and in this way you will fulfill the law of Christ. If anyone thinks he is something when he is nothing, he deceives himself. Each one should test his own actions. Then he can take pride in himself, without comparing himself to somebody else, for each one should carry his own load" (Galatians 6:1-5).

▮▮▮ Inappropriate Interaction

"A gossip betrays a confidence; so avoid a man who talks too much" (Proverbs 20:19).

▮▮▮ Speaking the Truth in Love

"A wise man's heart guides his mouth, and his lips promote instruction" (Proverbs 16:23).

"Better is open rebuke than hidden love" (Proverbs 27:5).

"He who rebukes a man will in the end gain more favor than he who has a flattering tongue" (Proverbs 28:23).

"Speaking the truth in love, we will in all things grow up into him who is the Head, that is, Christ. From him the whole body, joined and held together by every supporting ligament, grows and builds itself up in love, as each part does its work" (Ephesians 4:15-16).

▮▮▮ Genuineness

"Why do you look at the speck of sawdust in your brother's eye and pay no attention to the plank in your own eye? How can you say to your brother, 'Brother, let me take the speck out of your eye,' when you yourself fail to see the plank in your own eye? You hypocrite, first take the plank out of your eye, and then you will see clearly to remove the speck from your brother's eye" (Luke 6:41-42).

▮▮▮ Change

"What, after all, is Apollos? And what is Paul? Only servants, through whom you came to believe—as the Lord has assigned to each his task. I planted the seed, Apollos watered it, but God made it grow. So neither he who plants nor he who waters is anything, but only God, who makes things grow. The man who plants and the man who waters have one purpose, and each will be rewarded according to his own labor. For we are God's fellow workers; you are God's field, God's building" (1 Corinthians 3:5-9).

▮▮▮ Confrontation

"Hatred stirs up dissension, but love covers all wrongs" (Proverbs 10:12).

"A patient man has great understanding, but a quick-tempered man displays folly" (Proverbs 14:29).

"A gentle answer turns away wrath, but a harsh word stirs up anger" (Proverbs 15:1).

"A hot-tempered man stirs up dissension, but a patient man calms a quarrel" (Proverbs 15:18).

"Better a patient man than a warrior, a man who controls his temper than one who takes a city" (Proverbs 16:32).

"A man of knowledge uses words with restraint, and a man of understanding is even-tempered" (Proverbs 17:27).

"Through patience a ruler can be persuaded, and a gentle tongue can break a bone" (Proverbs 25:15).

"Do not be quickly provoked in your spirit, for anger resides in the lap of fools" (Ecclesiastes 7:9).

"Brothers, if someone is caught in a sin, you who are spiritual should restore him gently. But watch yourself, or you also may be tempted" (Galatians 6:1).

"Instead, speaking the truth in love, we will in all things grow up into him who is the Head, that is, Christ" (Ephesians 4:15).

▌▌▌ Immediacy

"The way of a fool seems right to him, but a wise man listens to advice" (Proverbs 12:15).

"A fool gives full vent to his anger, but a wise man keeps himself under control" (Proverbs 29:11).

"Do not let any unwholesome talk come out of your mouths, but only what is helpful for building others up according to their needs, that it may benefit those who listen" (Ephesians 4:29).

▌▌▌ Listening to God

"May the words of my mouth and the meditation of my heart be pleasing in your sight, O Lord, my Rock and my Redeemer" (Psalm 19:14).

"But whoever listens to me will live in safety and be at ease, without fear of harm" (Proverbs 1:33).

"For the Lord gives wisdom and from his mouth come knowledge and understanding" (Proverbs 2:6).

"Now then, my sons, listen to me; do not turn aside from what I say" (Proverbs 5:7).

"Now then, my sons, listen to me; blessed are those who keep my ways" (Proverbs 8:32).

"Blessed is the man who listens to me" (Proverbs 8:34a).

"To man belong the plans of the heart, but from the Lord comes the reply of the tongue" (Proverbs 16:1).

"Every word of God is flawless; he is a shield to those who take refuge in him" (Proverbs 30:5).

"Guard your steps when you go to the house of God. Go near to listen rather than to offer the sacrifice of fools, who do not know that they do wrong.

"Do not be quick with your mouth, do not be hasty in your heart to utter anything before God. God is in heaven and you are on earth, so let your words be few" (Ecclesiastes 5:1-2).

Resources

Briner, Bob and Pritchard, Ray, *The Leadership Lessons of Jesus: A Timeless Model for Today's Leaders.* Nashville, TN: Broadman & Holman Publishers, 1997.

Covey, Stephen R., *The Seven Habits of Highly Effective People: Restoring the Character Ethic.* New York, NY: Fireside, 1990.

Crabb, Larry, *Connecting: Healing for Ourselves and Our Relationships: A Radical New Vision.* Nashville, TN: Word Publishing, 1997.

Dodd, Brian J., *Empowered Church Leadership: Ministry in the Spirit According to Paul.* Downers Grove, IL: InterVarsity Press, 2003.

Eyre, Stephen D., *Drawing Close to God: The Essentials of a Dynamic Quiet Time.* Downers Grove, IL: InterVarsity Press, 1995.

Goleman, Daniel, *Emotional Intelligence.* New York, NY: Bantam Books, 1995.

Heitler, Susan, *From Conflict to Resolution: Skills and Strategies for Individual, Couple, and Family Therapy.* New York, NY: W.W. Norton & Company, Inc., 1990.

Herniss, Cary and Goleman, Daniel, eds., *The Emotionally Intelligent Workplace.* San Francisco, CA: John Wiley & Sons, Inc., 2001.

Huggett, Joyce, *The Joy of Listening to God: Hearing the Many Ways God Speaks to Us.* Downers Grove, IL: InterVarsity Press, 1987.

Jones, Laurie Beth, *Jesus, CEO: Using Ancient Wisdom for Visionary Leadership.* New York, NY: Hyperion, 1995.

Lencioni, Patrick, *The Five Dysfunctions of a Team: A Leadership Fable.* San Francisco, CA: Jossey-Bass, 2002.

Lucado, Max, *It's Not About Me.* Nashville, TN: Integrity Publishers, 2004.

Maxwell, John C,. *Developing the Leaders Around You: How to Help Others Reach Their Full Potential.* Nashville, TN: Thomas Nelson Publishers, 2003.

Nouwen, Henri J. M., *Life of the Beloved: Spiritual Living in a Secular World.* New York, NY: The Crossroad Publishing Company, 1992.

Ross, Alan M., and Murphey, Cecil, *Unconditional Excellence: Answering God's Call to Be Your Professional Best.* Avon, MA: Adams Media Corporation, 2002.

Sweeten, Gary; Ping, Dave; and Clippard, Anne, *Listening for Heaven's Sake: Building Healthy Relationships With God, Self and Others.* Cincinnati, OH: Teleios Publications, 1993.

Swindoll, Charles R., *Intimacy With the Almighty.* Dallas, TX: J. Countryman, 1999.

Vella, Jane, *Learning to Listen, Learning to Teach: The Power of Dialogue in Educating Adults.* San Francisco, CA: John Wiley & Sons, Inc., 2002.